KB086901

Grammar Joy
중등 영문법

2a

POLY BOOKS

저자 **이 종 저**

이화여자대학교 졸업
Longman Grammar Joy 1, 2, 3, 4권
Longman Vocabulary Mentor Joy 1, 2, 3권
I am Grammar 1, 2권
Grammar & Writing Level A 1, 2권 / Level B 1, 2권
Polybooks Grammar joy start 1, 2권
Polybooks Grammar joy 1, 2, 3, 4권
Polybooks Grammar joy 중등 영문법 1a,1b,2a,2b,3a,3b권
Polybooks 문법을 잡아주는 영작 1, 2, 3, 4권
Polybooks Grammar joy & Writing 1, 2, 3, 4권
Polybooks Bridging 초등 Voca 1, 2권
Polybooks Joy 초등 Voca [phonics words] 1, 2권

저자 **박 영 교**

서울대학교 졸업
前 강남 IVY 영어학원 대표 원장
Polybooks Grammar joy 중등 영문법 1a,1b,2a,2b,3a,3b권
길벗스쿨 한 문장 영어독해 무작정 따라하기

감수 **Jeanette Lee**

Wellesley college 졸업

Grammar Joy 중등 영문법 2a

지은이 | 이종저, 박영교
펴낸곳 | POLY books
펴낸이 | POLY 영어 교재 연구소
기 획 | 박정원
편집디자인 | 박혜영

초판 1쇄 인쇄 | 2015년 10월 30일
초판 20쇄 인쇄 | 2023년 4월 15일

POLY 영어 교재 연구소
경기도 성남시 분당구 황새울로 200번길 28 (수내동, 오너스타워)
전 화 070-7799-1583 Fax (031) 262-1583

ISBN l 979-11-86924-80-8
        979-11-86924-77-8 (세트)

Grammar Joy
중등 영문법

2a

POLY BOOKS

Preface

먼저 그 동안 Grammar Joy Plus를 아껴 주시고 사랑해 주신 분들께 감사를 드립니다. 본 책의 저자는 Grammar Joy Plus를 직접 출간하게 되었습니다. 저자가 직접 출간하게 된 만큼 더 많은 정성과 노력을 들여 미흡하였던 기존의 Grammar Joy Plus를 완전 개정하고 내신문제를 추가하였으며, 책 제목을 Grammar Joy 중등영문법으로 바꾸어 여러분께 선보이게 되었습니다.

모든 교재에서 키포인트는 저자가 학생들의 눈높이를 아는 것입니다. 같은 내용의 문법을 공부하더라도 그 내용을 저자가 어떻게 쉽게 풀어 나가느냐 하는 것이 가장 중요하며, 이에 비중을 두어 만든 교재야말로 최상의 교재라고 생각합니다. Grammar Joy 중등영문법은 저희가 오랜 현장 경험을 바탕으로 이 부분에 초점을 맞추어 만들었습니다.

첫째, 본 교재는 비록 처음 접하는 어려운 내용의 문법일지라도 학생들에게 쉽게 학습효과를 얻을 수 있도록 설명하였습니다. 학생들이 small step으로 진행하면서 학습 목표에 도달할 수 있도록 쉬운 내용부터 시작하여 어려운 내용까지 단계별로 구성하였습니다.

둘째, 시각적으로 용이하게 인식할 수 있도록 문제의 틀을 만들었습니다. 문장의 구조를 도식화하여 설명과 문제 유형을 만들었으므로, 어렵고 복잡한 내용도 쉽게 이해하고 기억에 오래 남을 수 있습니다.

셋째, 쉬운 단어로 구성했습니다. 학습자들이 문장 중에 어려운 단어가 많으면 정작 배워야 할 문법에 치중하지 못하고 싫증을 내고 맙니다. 따라서 학습자 누구나 단어로 인한 어려움 없이 공부할 수 있도록 단어를 선별하였습니다.

넷째, 생동감 있는 문장들을 익힐 수 있도록 하였습니다. 실생활에서 사용되어지는 문장들을 가지고 공부함으로써 현장에 적용시킬 수 있습니다.

다섯째, 풍부한 양의 문제를 제공합니다. 최대의 학습 효과를 얻기 위해서는 학생 스스로가 공부하는 시간을 많이 가지는 것입니다. 또한 많은 문제를 제공함으로 학생 스스로 문제를 풀어 가면서 문법 내용을 본인도 모르는 사이에 저절로 실력 향상을 이룰 수 있습니다.

본 교재를 비롯하여 Grammar Joy Start, Grammar Joy, Grammar Joy 중등영문법을 연계하여 공부한다면 Grammar는 완벽하게 이루어질 것입니다.

특히 저자가 직접 출간한 교재는 타사의 본 교재를 흉내낸 교재들이 따라 올 수 없는 차이점을 느끼실 수 있습니다. 아무쪼록 이 시리즈를 통하여 여러분의 영어 공부에 많은 발전이 있기를 바라며 함께 고생해 주신 박혜영, 박정원께도 감사를 드립니다.

저자 이종거 박영교

Contents

Series Contents

Guide to **This Book**

이 책의 구성과 특징을 파악하고 본 책을 최대한 여러분의 시간에 맞춰 공부 계획을 세워 보세요.

1 Unit별 핵심정리

예비 중학생들이 반드시 알아 두어야 할 문법들을 체계적으로 간단 명료하게 unit별로 정리하였습니다.

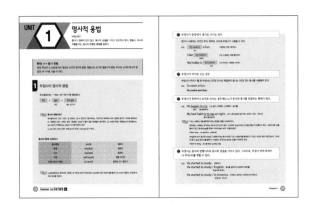

2 핵심 정리

좀 더 심화된 문법을 배우기전 이미 학습한 내용을 정리하여 쉽게 복습할 수 있도록 하였습니다.

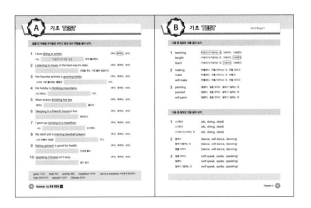

3 기초 test

각 unit별 필수 문법을 잘 이해하고 있는지 기초적인 문제로 짚어 보도록 합니다.

4 기본 test

기초 test 보다 좀 더 어려운 문제를 풀어 봄으로써 핵심 문법에 좀 더 접근해 가도록 하였습니다.

5

실력 test

좀 더 심화된 문제를 통하여 문법을 완성시켜
주도록 하였습니다.

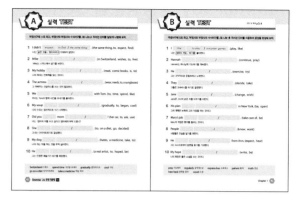

6

내신대비

지금까지 배운 내용을 내신에 적용할 수 있도록
문제 유형을 구성하였고 이를 통해 시험 대비
능력을 키울 수 있도록 하였습니다.

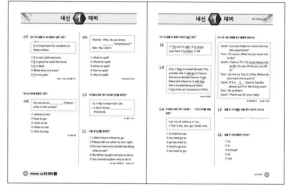

7

종합 문제

본 책에서 공부한 내용을 총괄하여 문제를 구
성하였으므로 이를 통하여 학습 성과를 평
가할 수 있습니다.

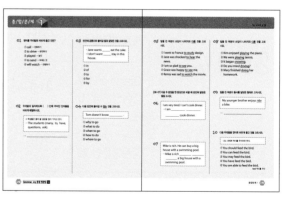

8

영단어 Quizbook

본 책의 학습에 필요한 단어들을 사전에 준
비시켜 어휘가 문법을 공부하는데 걸림돌이
되지 않도록 하고 학생들의 어휘 실력을 향상
시킬 수 있도록 준비하였습니다.

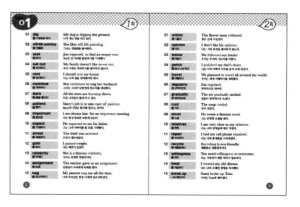

How to Use This Book

Grammar Joy 중등영문법 Series는 총 6권으로 각 권당 6주 총 6개월의 수업 분량으로 이루어져 있습니다. 학생들의 학업 수준과 능력, 그리고 학습 시간에 따라 각 테스트를 과제로 주어 교육 과정 조정이 가능합니다. 아래에 제시한 학습계획표를 참고로 학교진도에 맞춰 부분적으로 선별하여 학습을 진행할 수도 있습니다.

Month	Course	Week	Hour	Part	Homework/ Extra
1st Month	Grammar Joy 중등영문법 1a	1st	1 2 3	문장의 구성 부정사 A	▶ chapter별 단어 test는 과제로 주어 수업 시작 전에 test
	Grammar Joy 중등영문법 1a	2nd	1 2 3	부정사 B 동명사	▶ 각 chapter별 내신대비는 과제로 주거나 각 chapter 수업 후 test
	Grammar Joy 중등영문법 1a	3rd	1 2 3	분사	
	Grammar Joy 중등영문법 1a	4th	1 2 3	조동사	
2nd Month	Grammar Joy 중등영문법 1a	1st	1 2 3	수동태	
	Grammar Joy 중등영문법 1a	2nd	1 2 3	현재완료	
	Grammar Joy 중등영문법 1b	3rd	1 2 3	명사와 관사	
	Grammar Joy 중등영문법 1b	4th	1 2 3	대명사	
3rd Month	Grammar Joy 중등영문법 1b	1st	1 2 3	형용사와 부사	
	Grammar Joy 중등영문법 1b	2nd	1 2 3	비교 전치사	
	Grammar Joy 중등영문법 1b	3rd	1 2 3	명사절과 상관 접속사	
	Grammar Joy 중등영문법 1b	4th	1 2 3	부사절	▶ 종합 test는 각 권이 끝난 후 evaluation 자료로 사용한다

Month	Course	Week	Hour	Part	Homework/Extra
4th Month	Grammar Joy 중등영문법 2a	1st	1 2 3	부정사 A	▶chapter별 단어 test는 과제로 주어 수업 시작 전에 test
	Grammar Joy 중등영문법 2a	2nd	1 2 3	부정사 B	▶각 chapter별 내신대비는 과제로 주거나 각 chapter 수업 후 test
	Grammar Joy 중등영문법 2a	3rd	1 2 3	동명사	
	Grammar Joy 중등영문법 2a	4th	1 2 3	분사 구문	
5th Month	Grammar Joy 중등영문법 2a	1st	1 2 3	조동사 수동태	
	Grammar Joy 중등영문법 2a	2nd	1 2 3	완료	
	Grammar Joy 중등영문법 2b	3rd	1 2 3	비교 명사절	
	Grammar Joy 중등영문법 2b	4th	1 2 3	부사절과 접속부사	
6th Month	Grammar Joy 중등영문법 2b	1st	1 2 3	관계대명사 A	
	Grammar Joy 중등영문법 2b	2nd	1 2 3	관계대명사 B	
	Grammar Joy 중등영문법 2b	3rd	1 2 3	시제의 일치와 화법	
	Grammar Joy 중등영문법 2b	4th	1 2 3	가정법	▶종합 test는 각 권이 끝난 후 evaluation 자료로 사용한다

Month	Course	Week	Hour	Part	Homework/Extra
7th Month	Grammar Joy 중등영문법 3a	1st	1 2 3	부정사	▶chapter별 단어 test는 과제로 주어 수업 시작 전에 test
	Grammar Joy 중등영문법 3a	2nd	1 2 3	동명사	▶각 chapter별 실전Test는 과제로 주거나 각 Chapter 수업 후 test
	Grammar Joy 중등영문법 3a	3rd	1 2 3	분사	
	Grammar Joy 중등영문법 3a	4th	1 2 3	분사구문	
8th Month	Grammar Joy 중등영문법 3a	1st	1 2 3	조동사	
	Grammar Joy 중등영문법 3a	2nd	1 2 3	수동태 명사와 관사	
	Grammar Joy 중등영문법 3b	3rd	1 2 3	대명사	
	Grammar Joy 중등영문법 3b	4th	1 2 3	형용사와 부사	
9th Month	Grammar Joy 중등영문법 3b	1st	1 2 3	비교	
	Grammar Joy 중등영문법 3b	2nd	1 2 3	관계사	
	Grammar Joy 중등영문법 3b	3rd	1 2 3	가정법	
	Grammar Joy 중등영문법 3b	4th	1 2 3	전치사 특수 구문	▶종합 Test는 각 권이 끝난 후 evaluation 자료로 사용한다

Chapter 1

부정사 A

부정사란?

'to + 동사원형'의 형태로 품사가 정해져 있지 않고, 동사의 성질을 가지고 있으면서
명사, 형용사, 부사의 역할을 하는 동사의 변형된 형태를 말한다.

🧊 명사적 용법

ⓐ 우리말에서는 '~하는 것(~하기)'에 해당한다.

- 주어역할　　*ex.* **To swim** in the river is dangerous. 강에서 수영하는 것은 위험하다.
- 목적어역할　*ex.* I want **to play** with Jane. 나는 Jane과 놀기를 원한다.
- 보어 역할　　*ex.* My hope is **to be** a dancer. 나의 희망은 무용수가 되는 것이다.

ⓑ '의문사 + to 부정사'는 아래와 같은 뜻을 가지고 있다.

ex. I don't know **what to say**.

what + to부정사　무엇을 ~ 해야할지,	when + to부정사　언제 ~해야할지,
where + to부정사　어디서 ~해야할지,	how + to부정사　어떻게 ~해야할지, ~하는 법

🧊 형용사적 용법

우리말에서는 '~할'에 해당한다.

- 명사 + to 부정사　　*ex.* I don't have time **to meet** you. 나는 너를 만날 시간이 없다.

🧊 부사적 용법

문장 내에서 to 부정사가 부사의 역할을 하는 경우를 말하며, 이 때 부정사는 기본 문장에 덧붙여 추가 정보를 제공하는 역할을 한다.

ⓐ 목적 : ~하기 위하여

ex. I entered the room **to take a test**. 나는 휴식을 취하기 위하여 방에 들어갔다

ⓑ 원인, 이유 : ~해서, ~때문에

ex. She was sad **to hear the news**. 그녀는 그 소식을 들어서 슬펐다.

ⓒ 결과 : ~해서....하다

ex. She grew up **to be a violinist**. 그녀는 자라서 (결국) 바이올리니스트가 되었다.

ⓓ 형용사 수식 : ~하기가

ex. This book is difficult **to understand**. 이 책은 이해하기가 어렵다.

ⓔ 판단 : ~하는 것을 보니

ex. He must be a fool **to say so**. 그는 그렇게 말하는 것을 보니 바보임에 틀림없다

1 명사적 용법

1 It~for (of)... to−

◆ It~for... to−

It~to....의 형태에서 부정사의 주어는 부정사 바로 앞에 'for + 목적격'을 써서 to 부정사의 주어를 나타내고 이를 '의미상의 주어'라고 한다.

ex. It is dangerous **to** swim in the sea. 바다에서 수영하는 것은 위험하다.

It is dangerous **for him to** swim in the sea. 그가 바다에서 수영하는 것은 위험하다.

Tip! 부정사는 그 근본이 동사에 뿌리를 두고 있기 때문에 동사의 성질을 가지고 있다. 따라서 영어의 어순은 '주어＋동사'의 형태이므로 to부정사의 주어는 부정사 바로 앞에 온다. 부정사의 주어라는 것을 나타내기 위해 부정사의 주어 앞에 for(of)를 넣어 준다.

◆ It~of... to−

칭찬이나 비난을 나타내는 형용사 뒤에는 'of + 목적격'을 써서 to 부정사의 의미상의 주어를 나타낸다.

ex. It is foolish **to** say so. 그렇게 말하는 것은 어리석다.

It is foolish **of her to** say so. 그녀가 그렇게 말하는 것은 어리석다.

칭찬 또는 비난을 나타내는 형용사

칭찬	kind, wise, smart, clever 영리한, polite 예의바른, careful 조심스러운, brave 용감한 ...
비난	foolish, stupid 어리석은, careless 부주의한, rude 무례한...

good과 nice
- good : '좋은'이라는 의미로 쓰이면 'for', '착한'이라는 의미로 쓰이면 'of'를 사용한다.
- nice : '멋진'이라는 의미로 쓰이면 'for', '친절한'이라는 의미로 쓰이면 'of'를 사용한다.

2 의문사 + to부정사

◆ '의문사 + to부정사'는 절로 바꿔 줄 수 있다.

의문사 + to 부정사 = 의문사 + 주어 + should~

ex. I don't know what **to** do. 나는 무엇을 해야 할지 모르겠다.

= I don't know what **I should** do.

의문사 + 주어 + should

주어진 문장을 우리말로 옮겨 보자.

1 It is easy for him to read the book.

그가 그 책을 읽는 것은   쉽다.

It is easy to read the book.

그 책을 읽는 것은   쉽다.

2 It is a great feeling for children to sleep in a tent.

대단한 느낌이다.

It is a great feeling to sleep in a tent.

대단한 느낌이다.

3 It is hard to say 'No.'

어렵다

It is hard for me to say 'No.'

어렵다

다음 중 알맞은 것을 골라 보자.

1 It is great for (they, them , their) to build the bridge.

2 It is difficult for (she, her, hers) to understand me.

3 It is impossible for (we, our, us) to climb Mt. Everest.

4 It is rude of (you, your, yours) to act like that.

5 It is important for (Jane, Jane's) to take medicine on time.

impossible 불가능한   Mt. Everest 에베레스트산

정답 및 해설 **p.2**

부정사의 의미상의 주어 앞에 올 수 있는 형용사들이다. 알맞은 형용사를 보기에서 골라 써 넣어 보자.

| 보기 |

kind	good 좋은	nice 멋진	safe	careless
polite	necessary	foolish	easy	possible
wise	important	careful	difficult	dangerous
rude	stupid	hard	smart	brave clever

1 It ~   *good*   + for 목적격 + to 부정사

2 It ~   + of 목적격 + to 부정사

–

necessary 필요한   safe 안전한   possible 가능한

다음 중 알맞은 것을 골라 보자.

1 It was impossible ((for), of) me to fly an airplane.

2 It was wise (for, of) them to follow his opinion.

3 It was kind (for, of) you to help the disabled.

4 It was brave (for, of) us to fight them.

5 It is difficult (for, of) her to fix the car.

6 It is important (for, of) him to meet your boss.

7 It is stupid (for, of) them to run away suddenly.

8 It is careful (for, of) you to treat him well.

9 It was fun (for, of) him to play baseball.

10 It was careless (for, of) me to break the flower pot.

11 It is dangerous (for, of) the child to cook ramyen.

12 It was boring (for, of) us to take her lesson.

13 It is smart (for, of) Mary to solve the quiz.

14 It is good (for, of) him to return to Korea.

15 It is nice (for, of) Ann to set a bird free.

---

fly (비행기를)조종하다   follow 따르다   opinion 의견   the disabled 장애인   suddenly 갑자기
treat 다루다   ramyon 라면   set~free ~를 놓아주다

다음 중 알맞은 것을 골라 보자.

1 It is kind (of, for) him to tell them the direction.

2 It is hard (of, for) me to study math.

3 It was clever (of, for) her to act like that.

4 It is difficult (of, for) him to have an interest in study.

5 It wasn't easy (of, for) him to get money.

6 It is possible (of, for) you to climb up the top of the tree.

7 It was exciting (of, for) us to watch a soccer game.

8 It is foolish (of, for) them to think of that deeply.

9 It was smart (of, for) Susan to do such a thing.

10 It was shocking (of, for) her to get a low grade on the exam.

11 It is surprising (of, for) the boys to find the treasure.

12 It is rude (of, for) you to speak loudly in the subway.

13 It was impossible (of, for) Min-su to guide the Americans.

14 It is brave (of, for) Tom to help the police officer.

15 It was right (of, for) him to take care of sick people.

---

direction 방향   have an interest in study 공부에 재미를 붙이다   treasure 보물   guide 안내하다

C 기본 TEST

다음 주어진 단어를 이용하여 알맞은 전치사와 함께 써 넣어 보자.

1 It is hard   *for me*   to fix the computer. (I)

2 It is kind   to show me the way. (he)

3 It is rude   to keep us waiting . (she)

4 It is necessary   to speak in English. (you)

5 It was foolish   to eat too much. (Jim)

6 It is difficult   to answer the question. (we)

7 It is polite   to listen to other people. (the girl)

8 It is expensive   to stay at the hotel. (they)

9 It is interesting   to like the super car. (Amy)

10 It is important   to have a dream. (he)

super car 초고성능 자동차

D 기본 TEST

정답 및 해설 **p.2**

다음 주어진 단어를 이용하여 알맞은 전치사와 함께 써 넣어 보자.

1 It is not safe *for you* to stay here. (you)

2 It is right to accept it today. (they)

3 It was brave to stand up to the bully. (James)

4 It is easy to do so. (I)

5 It was good to make a reservation at the W hotel. (she)

6 It is necessary to prepare for the flood. (we)

7 It is wrong to tell a lie. (you)

8 It was impossible to get along with Jim. (he)

9 It was wise to say sorry to her friend. (she)

10 It is dangerous to follow a stranger. (children)

accept 받아들이다　　stand up to ~에게 맞서다　　bully 불량배　　make a reservation 예약하다
prepare for ~대비하다　　flood 홍수　　show ... the way ...에게 길을 가르쳐 주다
get along with ~와 잘 지내다　　stranger 낯선 사람

의미상의 주어와 진주어에 O표 하고, 우리말에 알맞게 문장을 완성해 보자.

1 It is possible *for the police officer* *to find out* Jenny.
(그 경찰관이) (Jenny를 찾는 것은) 가능하다.

2 for monkeys trees.
원숭이들이 나무에 오르는 것은 쉽다.

3 It is brave a tiger.
그가 호랑이를 포획하는 것은 용맹스러운 일이다.

4 to take care of sick people.
그들이 아픈 사람들을 돌보는 것은 착한 일이다.

5 of Tom before meal.
Tom이 식사 전에 손을 씻는 것은 예의가 바른 것이다.

6 to trust the man.
Mary가 그 남자를 신뢰하는 것은 어리석었다.

7 It is unnecessary all the recipes.
요리사가 모든 조리법을 외우는 것은 필요없는 일이다.

8 It is unusal celebrities.
우리가 연예인들을 만나는 것은 드물다.

9 to fall on the escalator.
네가 에스컬레이터에서 넘어지는 것은 부주의한 것이다.

10 It is necessary a ticket now.
그녀는 지금 표를 사는 것이 필요하다.

---

climb up 오르다   capture 포획하다   recipe 조리법   memorize 외우다   celebrity 연예인   unusal 드문

의미상의 주어와 진주어에 ○표 하고, 우리말에 알맞게 문장을 완성해 보자.

1 It was kind *of Tom* *to be* with you.

　Tom이　너와 함께 있어주는 것은　친절한 일이었다.

2 _____ to win a gold medal.

그들이 금메달을 따는 것은 놀라운 일이다.

3 _____ for me _____ hot peppers.

내가 매운 고추를 먹는 것은 불가능하다.

4 It is wrong _____ the meeting.

나의 상사가 회의를 연기하는 것은 잘못된 것이다.

5 _____ for Bill _____ the drum.

Bill이 드럼을 연주하는 것은 멋지다.

6 _____ to eat fast food everyday.

나의 아들이 매일 패스트푸드를 먹는 것은 끔찍하다.

7 _____ to waste time with Jane.

그녀가 Jane과 빈둥거리는 것은 어리석다.

8 It was brave _____ the baby in the fire.

그 소방관이 불속에서 그 아기를 구조한 것은 용감한 것이었다.

9 It is important _____ to the school in time.

학생들이 학교에 제 시간에 도착하는 것은 중요하다.

10 _____ of you _____ a knife safely.

네가 칼을 안전하게 사용하는 것은 현명하다.

---

hot pepper 매운 고추　　put off 연기하다　　drum 북/드럼　　terrible 끔찍한　　waste time 빈둥거리다
rescue 구조하다　　get to ~에 도착하다

A 실력 TEST

부정사를 절로 바꾸어 같은 표현으로 만들어 보자.

1 She didn't know what to do.

= She didn't know *what she should do* .

2 He decided where to live.

= He decided _____ .

3 My sister didn't know what to say.

= My sister didn't know _____ .

4 They didn't decide when to leave here.

= They didn't decide _____ here.

5 Frank wonders how to save his money.

= Frank wonders _____ his money.

절을 부정사로 바꾸어 같은 표현으로 만들어 보자.

1 She asked how she should get there.

= She asked *how to get there* .

2 My mom didn't decide when she should go surfing.

= My mom didn't decide _____ surfing.

3 I planned what I should sell this year.

= I planned _____ this year.

4 We are planning where we should go on a trip.

= We are planning _____ a trip.

5 Ted asked when he should call me again.

= Ted asked _____ me again.

go surfing 서핑하다

실력 TEST

정답 및 해설 p.3

부정사와 절을 이용하여 우리말에 알맞게 문장을 완성해 보자.

1 나는 올해 무엇을 배워야 할지를 생각하고 있었다.

= I was thinking _what to learn_ this year.

= I was thinking _what I should learn_ this year.

2 Sally는 소고기를 어떻게 요리해야 하는지를(요리하는 법을) 배웠다.

= Sally learned _____ the beef.

= Sally learned _____ the beef.

3 언제 너의 집에 들러야 하는지 말해줘.

= Tell me _____ your house.

= Tell me _____ your house.

4 그 말들은 어디서 풀을 뜯어 먹어야 할지를 모른다.

= The horses didn't know _____ on grass.

= The horses didn't know _____ on grass.

5 John은 거기에서 무엇을 사야할지 고민 중이다.

= John is considering _____ there.

= John is considering _____ there.

6 그는 어떻게 자전거를 타야 하는지(자전거 타는 법) 알고 있다.

= He knows _____ a bike.

= He knows _____ a bike.

---

call at 들르다   **feed on grass** 풀을 뜯어먹다

UNIT

2 형용사적 용법

1 ~thing + 형용사 + to 부정사

> 💠 '~thing + 형용사'와, '~thing + to 부정사', '~thing + 형용사 + to 부정사'

~thing + 형용사

~thing으로 끝나는 부정대명사(something, anything, everything, nothing)를 꾸며주는 형용사는 부정대명사 뒤에 온다.

ex. I want something cold. 나는 차가운 (어떤) 것을 원한다.

~thing + to 부정사

ex. I want something to drink. 나는 마실 (어떤) 것을 원한다.

~thing + 형용사 + to 부정사

~thing으로 끝나는 부정대명사를 형용사와 to 부정사가 함께 수식할 때의 어순은 '~thing + 형용사' 뒤에 to 부정사를 붙여주면 된다.

ex. I want something cold to drink. 나는 마실 차가운 (어떤) 것을 원한다.

주어진 대명사를 사용하여 우리말을 영어로 옮겨 보자.

1 anything

달콤한 / (어떤) 것	*anything*	*sweet*	×
먹을 / (어떤) 것	*anything*	×	*to eat*
먹을 / 달콤한 / (어떤) 것	*anything*	*sweet*	*to eat*

2 something

특별한 / (어떤) 것

사야 할 / 특별한 / (어떤) 것

사야 할 / (어떤) 것

3 everything

배워야 할 / 중요한 / 모든 것

배워야 할 / 모든 것

중요한 / 모든 것

4 nothing

새로운 / 아무것도

알아야 할 / 새로운 / 아무것도

알아야 할 / 아무 것도

special 특별한   important 중요한

주어진 단어들을 우리말에 알맞게 나열해 보자.

1 Carving is *something difficult to learn* alone.
(to, something, learn, difficult)
조각은 혼자 배우기 어려운 것이다.

2 They have to the party.
(unique, to, something, bring)
그들은 파티에 가져갈 독특한 (어떤) 것이 있다.

3 I don't want at my home.
(to, anything , happen)
나는 내 집에서 아무 일도 일어나지 않길 원한다.

4 He needs in winter.
(to, wear, something)
그는 겨울에 입을 (어떤) 것이 좀 필요하다.

5 I have about Ann.
(nothing, to, say, special)
나는 Ann에 대해 말할 특별한 것이 아무 것도 없다.

6 She had in her studio.
(clear up, to, something)
그녀는 그녀의 스튜디오에 정리해야할 것이 있었다.

7 Did you find in the place?
(anything, unusual)
너는 그 장소에서 특이한 (어떤) 것을 발견했니?

8 Sam has for lunch.
(light, something, eat, to)
Sam은 점심에 먹을 가벼운 (어떤) 것을 좀 가지고 있다.

carve 조각하다   happen 일어나다   unusal 특이한, 흔치않은

우리말의 ~thing, 형용사, 부정사를 ○표 한 후, 주어진 단어를 이용하여 문장을 완성해 보자.

1 I want   *something warm to eat*   with her. (warm)

나는 그녀와 먹을 따뜻한 (어떤) 것을 원한다.

2 The old lady cannot chew   . (hard)

그 할머니는 딱딱한 (어떤) 것도 씹을 수 없다.

3 He has   . (sweet)

그는 달콤한 (어떤) 것을 가지고 있다.

4 She didn't want   . (watch, fun)

그녀는 볼 재미있는 (어떤) 것을 원하지 않았다.

5 We bought   . (necessary)

우리는 필요한 모든 것을 샀다.

6 I borrowed   . (read, interesting)

나는 읽을 흥미로운 (어떤) 것을 빌렸다.

7 The book contains   . (hard, understand)

그 책은 이해하기 어려운 아무 것도 없다.

8 Rachel chose   him. (nice, give)

Rachel은 그에게 줄 멋진 (어떤) 것을 골랐다.

9 That's   . (rare)

그것은 드문 (어떤) 일이다.

10 Did he bring   ? (important)

그는 중요한 (어떤) 것이라도 가져왔니?

---

contain (담고) 있다, 포함하다   rare 드문

UNIT 3 부사적 용법

1. too... to~ 너무 ...해서 ~할 수 없다.

ex. This coffee is **too** hot **to** drink. 이 커피는 너무 뜨거워서 마실 수 없다.

의미상의 주어

문장의 주어와 to부정사의 주어가 같은 경우

ex. **He** is too young **to** go to school. (he =go) 그는 너무 어려서 학교에 갈수 없다.

문장의 주어와 to부정사의 주어가 다른 경우 'for + 목적격'을 to부정사 앞에 써주면 된다.

ex. **This coffee** is too hot **for me** to drink fast. (me = drink)
이 커피는 너무 뜨거워서 내가 빨리 마실 수 없다.

too ~ to....를 절로 바꾸어 줄 수 있다.

> too~to.... = so~that 주어 cannot....

문장의 주어와 to부정사의 주어가 같은 경우

ex. I am **too** busy **to** go to the seminar. 나는 너무 바빠서 그 세미나에 갈 수 없다.
   = I am **so** busy **that** I **cannot** go to the seminar.

문장의 주어와 to부정사의 주어가 다른 경우: 문장의 주어(the cap)를 목적격 대명사(it)로 바꾸어 추가한다.

ex. **The cap** is too big **for him** to wear. 그 모자는 너무 커서 그는 쓸 수가 없다.
   = **The cap** is so big that **he** cannot wear **it**.

• 주어가 일반명사일 때 앞에 나오는 주어를 대명사로 받는다.
   ex. My brother is too honest to tell a lie.
      = **My brother** is so honest that **he** cannot tell a lie.

• 시제가 과거일 때는 can 대신 could를 사용한다.
   ex. She was too tired to do her homework.
      = She **was** so tired that she **could** not do her homework.

2 **....enough to~** ~하기에(~할 수 있을 만큼) 충분히 ...하다

ex. He studied hard **enough to** pass the exam.

그는 그 시험에 통과할 수 있을 만큼 충분히 열심히 공부했다

의미상의 주어

문장의 주어와 to부정사의 주어가 같은 경우

ex. **He** is old enough **to** go to school. (he = go) 그는 학교에 갈 만큼 충분히 나이가 들었다.

문장의 주어와 to부정사의 주어가 다른 경우 'for + 목적격'을 to부정사 앞에 써주면 된다.

ex. **This room** is big enough **for ten boys** to sleep in. (ten boys = sleep)

이 방은 10명의 소년들이 잘 수 있을 만큼 충분히 크다.

(이 방은 충분히 커서 10명의 소년들이 잘 수 있다.)

'~enough to...'를 절로 바꾸어 줄 수 있다.

~enough to.... = so~that 주어 can....

문장의 주어와 to부정사의 주어가 같은 경우

ex. He is strong **enough to** carry the bag. 그는 그 가방을 나르기에 충분히 힘이 세다.

= He is **so** strong **that** he **can** carry the bag.

문장의 주어와 to부정사의 주어가 다른 경우: 문장의 주어(the bag)를 목적격 대명사(it)로 바꾸어 추가한다.

ex. The bag is light enough **for her** to carry. 그 가방은 그녀가 나를 수 있을 만큼 충분히 가볍다.

= The bag is **so** light **that she can** carry it.

• 앞에 나오는 주어는 대명사로 받는다.

　ex. My sister is old enough to go to school.

　　= **My sister** is so old that **she** can go to school.

• 시제가 과거일 때는 can 대신 **could**를 사용한다.

　ex. She was rich enough to pay for the car.

　　= She **was** so rich that she **could** pay for the car.

의미상의 주어를 찾아 ○표시 한 후, 우리말로 옮겨 보자.

1 History is interesting enough to learn.

역사는　　　　　　　배우기에 충분히 재미있다　　　　　　.

History is interesting enough (for me) to learn.

역사는　　　　　　　내가 배우기에 충분히 재미있다　　　　　　.

2 This river is too dangerous to swim in.

이 강은　　　　　　　　　　　　　　　　　　　　　　.

This river is too dangerous for children to swim in.

이 강은　　　　　　　　　　　　　　　　　　　　　　.

3 His lesson is easy enough to understand.

그의 강의는　　　　　　　　　　　　　　　　　　　　.

His lesson is easy enough for me to understand.

그의 강의는　　　　　　　　　　　　　　　　　　　　.

4 The bridge is strong enough to cross.

그 다리는　　　　　　　　　　　　　　　　　　　　　.

The bridge is strong enough for trucks to cross.

그 다리는　　　　　　　　　　　　　　　　　　　　　.

5 This tunnel is too narrow to pass through.

이 터널은　　　　　　　　　　　　　　　　　　　　　.

This tunnel is too narrow for the bus to pass through.

이 터널은　　　　　　　　　　　　　　　　　　　　　.

---

cross 건너가다　　tunnel 터널　　narrow 좁은　　pass through 통과하다

주어진 문장의 시제를 고르고, 알맞은 것을 골라 보자.

1 Bill walked too slow to arrive there on time. (현재, 과거)
= Bill walked so slow that (he, Bill)(can't, couldn't) arrive there on time.

2 He is too ugly to catch the girl's eyes. (현재, 과거)
= He is so ugly that (she, he) (can't, couldn't) catch the girl's eyes.

3 The beggars were too poor to go to hospital. (현재, 과거)
= The beggars were so poor that (he, they) (can't, couldn't) go to hospital.

4 Susan was healthy enough to work all nights. (현재, 과거)
= Susan was so healthy that (Susan, she) (can, could) work all nights.

5 You and I are young enough to stand it. (현재, 과거)
= You and I are so young that (we, they) (can, could) stand it.

주어진 문장의 시제를 고르고, 알맞은 것을 골라 보자.

1 The box was too heavy for me to lift. (현재, 과거)
= The box was so heavy that (it, I)(can't, couldn't) lift it.

2 This watch is cheap enough for Jim to buy. (현재, 과거)
= This watch is so cheap that (he, Jim)(can, could) buy it.

3 The knife was too sharp for children to handle. (현재, 과거)
= The knife was so sharp that (they, children)(can't, couldn't) handle it.

4 The store is bright enough for him to read a brand in. (현재, 과거)
= The store is so bright that (she, he)(can, could) read a brand in it.

5 The job was too difficult for her to manage. (현재, 과거)
= The job was so difficult that (he, she) (can't, couldn't) manage it.

beggar 거지   stand 견디다   bright 밝은   brand 상표   manage 관리하다

두 문장이 같은 뜻이 되도록 문장을 완성해 보자.

1 I felt too lazy to go out.

= I felt   *so*   lazy   *that*   I   *couldn't*   go out.

2 Mary was kind enough to pick me up on her way home.

= Mary was so kind ▨▨▨▨▨▨▨▨▨▨▨▨▨ pick me up on her way home.

3 Tom is bold enough to do it.

= Tom is ▨▨▨▨▨▨ bold ▨▨▨▨▨▨▨▨▨▨▨▨▨ do it.

4 She was too sick to speak more.

= She was ▨▨▨▨▨▨▨▨▨▨ that ▨▨▨▨▨▨▨▨ speak more.

5 We were lucky enough to have a great teacher.

= We were so ▨▨▨▨▨▨▨▨ we ▨▨▨▨▨▨ have a great teacher.

6 This airplane is fast enough to fly 800km in an hour.

= This airplane is ▨▨▨▨▨ fast that ▨▨▨▨▨▨▨▨ fly 800km in an hour.

7 My boyfriend is too nervous to eat anything.

= My boyfriend is so nervous ▨▨▨▨▨▨▨▨▨▨▨▨ eat anything.

8 My brother was too sick to get out of bed.

= My brother was so ▨▨▨▨▨▨ that ▨▨▨▨▨▨▨▨ get out of bed.

9 Jenny was skinny enough to be a model.

= Jenny was so skinny that ▨▨▨▨▨▨▨▨▨ be a model.

10 She was too short to take a bumper car.

= She was ▨▨▨▨▨ short ▨▨▨▨ she ▨▨▨▨▨ take a bumper car.

---

lazy 게으른, 나른한   **bold** 용감한, 대담한   **bumper car** 범퍼카

부정사를 절로 바꾸어 같은 표현으로 만들어 보자.

1 He is good enough to be a director.

= He is   *so good that he can be*   a director.

2 She is rich enough to travel around the world.

= She is   around the world.

3 Joe was too hungry to walk farther.

= Joe was   farther.

4 I started too late to attend the meeting in time.

= I started   the meeting in time.

5 Paul is strong enough to work day and night.

= Paul is   day and night.

의미상의 주어에 ○표 하고, 부정사를 절로 바꾸어 같은 표현으로 만들어 보자.

1 This cake was too sweet (for him) to eat.

= This cake was   *so sweet that he couldn't eat*   it.

2 The tree is too tall for me to climb up to the top.

= The tree is   it up to the top.

3 Her income is much enough for her to buy a nice apartment with.

= Her income is   a nice apartment with it.

4 This super car was too expensive for Billy to purchase.

= This super car was   it.

5 The song is popular enough to be famous soon.

= The song is   famous soon.

---

director 감독   **farther** 더 멀리   **attend** 참석하다   **income** 수입   **apartment** 아파트
purchase 구입하다

기본 TEST

절을 부정사로 바꾸어 같은 표현으로 만들어 보자.

1 Nancy dances so well that she can win the first prize.

= Nancy dances _well enough to win_ the first prize.

2 He is so busy that he cannot meet his friends.

= He is _____ his friends.

3 Mom is so patient that she can listen to me anytime.

= Mom is _____ to me anytime.

4 The boy was so short that he couldn't push the button.

= The boy was _____ the button.

5 I am so lucky that I can have a good teacher.

= I am _____ a good teacher.

절을 부정사로 바꾸어 같은 표현으로 만들어 보자.

1 The boat is so big that we can get in it.

= The boat is _big enough for us to get_ in.

2 The train ran so fast that he couldn't stand on it.

= The train ran _____ on.

3 The riddle was so complex that I couldn't solve it.

= The riddle was _____ .

4 The schoolbag is so big that she can put her books in it.

= The schoolbag is _____ her books in.

5 The earrings were so small that Jane couldn't find them.

= The earrings were _____ .

---

patient 인내심이 있는   **push** 밀다, 누르다   **button** 단추   **complex** 복잡한   **textbook** 교과서

D 기본 TEST

주어진 단어를 이용하여 우리말에 알맞게 부정사와 절로 완성해 보자.

1 우리는 너무 흥분해서 소파위에 앉아 있을 수가 없었다. (excited)

→ We were *too excited to sit* on the sofa.

→ We were *so excited that we couldn't sit* on the sofa.

2 나는 충분히 키가 커서 전구를 바꿀 수 있다. (tall)

→ I am the light bulb.

→ I am the light bulb.

3 그녀는 너무 바빠서 전화를 받을 수가 없었다. (busy)

→ She was the phone.

→ She was the phone.

4 Joe는 너무 오줌이 마려워서 (심하게 오줌을 누고 싶어) 휴식시간을 기다릴 수 없다. (badly)

→ Joe needs to pee for the break.

→ Joe needs to pee for the break.

5 그는 은퇴할 만큼 충분히 나이가 들었다. (old)

→ He is .

→ He is .

6 John은 그것을 시도할 만큼 충분히 용감했다. (brave)

→ John was some of that.

→ John was some of that.

---

change 바꾸다   **light bulb** 전구   **pick up the phone** 전화를 받다   **pee** 오줌을 누다   **badly** 심하게
retire 은퇴하다

의미상의 주어를 ○표 하고, 주어진 단어를 이용하여 우리말에 알맞게 부정사와 절로 완성해 보자.

1 이 신발은 충분히 말라서(건조해서) 나의 아들이 신을 수 있다. (dry)

→ These shoes are *dry enough for my son to wear* .

→ These shoes are *so dry that my son can wear them* .

2 이 모자는 너무 작아서 그녀가 쓸 수가 없었다. (small)

→ This cap was .

→ This cap was .

3 그 개울은 너무 깊어 그 소년들이 들어가서 놀 수 없다. (deep)

→ The stream is .

→ The stream is .

4 이 약은 너무 써서 설탕없이는 내가 먹을 수 없었다. (bitter)

→ This medicine was without sugar.

→ This medicine was without sugar.

5 복숭아들이 충분히 익어서 농부들이 딸 수 있다. (ripe)

→ The peaches are .

→ The peaches are .

6 그 공들은 충분히 커서 아기들이 가지고 놀 수 있다. (big)

→ These balls are .

→ These balls are .

handle 다루다   take (약을) 먹다   ripe 익은

[01–02] 다음 빈칸에 알맞은 것을 고르시오.

01

> It is very difficult _____ to do the job by yourself.

① of you
② by you
③ from you
④ for you
⑤ to you

02

> It was kind _____ to say that.

① of she
② of her
③ from her
④ for her
⑤ to she

03 다음 빈칸에 알맞지 <u>않은</u> 것을 고르시오.

> It was _____ of him to go with them.

① wise
② stupid
③ important
④ foolish
⑤ careless

04 두 문장의 뜻이 같도록 빈칸에 알맞은 말을 고르시오.

> She knows where to go next year.
> = She knows where _____ next year.

① she goes
② she went
③ she can go
④ she should go
⑤ she would go

05 두 문장의 뜻이 같도록 빈칸에 알맞은 말을 쓰시오.

> Tom didn't know how to ride a bike.
> = Tom didn't know _____ _____ a bike.

06 우리말에 맞게 ( ) 안의 단어를 알맞게 배열한 것을 고르시오.

> 나는 먹을 단 어떤 것을(것을 좀) 샀다.
> = I bought (eat, to, sweet, something).

① sweet something to eat
② to eat sweet something
③ something sweet to eat
④ something to eat sweet
⑤ to eat something sweet

[07-08] 다음 빈칸에 들어갈 알맞은 말을 고르시오.

07

> Tom is too tired to go now.
> = Tom is _____ tired that he can't go now.

① too
② so
③ enough
④ the
⑤ to

08

> He is so smart that he can answer this question.
> = He is smart _____ to answer this question.
>
> 그는 그 질문에 대답할 수 있을 만큼 충분히 영리하다.

① so
② not
③ enough
④ and
⑤ too

09 다음 문장과 의미가 같은 것은?

> Tommy was lucky enough to win a free ticket.

① Tommy was not lucky, so he can win a free ticket.
② Tommy was so lucky, but he can win a free ticket.
③ Tommy was lucky because he can win a free ticket.
④ Tommy was so lucky that he could win a free ticket.
⑤ He can win a free ticket. though Tommy was lucky.

10 어법상 어색한 부분을 차례대로 알맞게 고른 것은?

> · My brother ⓐ is ⓑ enough old ⓒ to go ⓓ to kindergarten.
> · She ⓐ is ⓑ weak too ⓒ to play ⓓ tennis.

① ⓐ - ⓑ
② ⓐ - ⓒ
③ ⓑ - ⓒ
④ ⓑ - ⓑ
⑤ ⓒ - ⓓ

kindergarten 유치원

11 다음 문장과 의미가 같은 것은?

> The subway was fast enough for me to get there on time.

① The subway was too fast that I could get there on time.
② The subway was so fast that I can get there on time.
③ The subway was so fast that I could get there on time.
④ The subway was too fast that I cannot get there on time.
⑤ The subway was very fast that I can get there on time.

[12–13] 다음에서 잘못된 부분을 찾아 바르게 고치시오.

12

> They have nothing to wear warm.
> 그들은 입을 따뜻한 어떤 것도 없다.

_____ → _____

13

> She doesn't need good anything to read tonight.
> 그녀는 오늘 밤 읽을 좋은 어떤 것도 필요없다.

_____ → _____

14 두 문장의 뜻이 같지 않은 것을 고르시오.

① This bag is small enough for her to carry.
= This bag is so small that she can't carry it.
② Bill is too young to understand his parents.
= Bill is so young that he can't understand his parents.
③ Mary is kind enough to help them.
= Mary is so kind that she can help them.
④ He is too tired to do his homework.
= He is so tired that he can't do his homework.
⑤ This tea is too hot for me to drink.
= This tea is so hot that I can't drink it.

15 어법상 어색한 것을 고르시오.

> Yesterday, I ① invited Tom ② to my home. He brought ③ some games. I gave ④ something to drink cold to him. We had a great time. I really ⑤ like him.

16 틀린 곳을 찾아 바르게 고치시오. (한 단어)

> Kate was too poor that pay for the phone bill.

_____ → _____

17 다음 빈칸에 들어갈 알맞은 말을 고르시오.

> Kate was so poor that she _____ pay for the phone bill.

① can
② can't
③ could
④ couldn't
⑤ wasn't

18 다음 빈칸에 들어갈 말로 알맞은 것을 고르시오.

> He was so strong that he _____ stand it.
> 그는 그것을 견뎌낼 만큼 충분히 강했다.

① can
② could
③ can't
④ couldn't
⑤ must

stand 견뎌내다

[19~20] 다음 대화를 읽고 물음에 답하시오.

> _Sarah_ : Can you help me move into my new apartment?
> _Paul_ : Of course. What do you want me to do?
> _Sarah_ : ⓐ The TV is too heavy for me to lift. Do you think you can lift it?
> _Paul_ : Let me try. Yes, it is fine. Where do you want me to put it?
> _Sarah_ : If it is ___ⓑ___ hard to handle, please put it in the living room.
> _Paul_ : No problem.
> _Sarah_ : Thank you for your help!

lift 들어올리다   handle 다루다   put 두다

19 밑줄 친 ⓐ와 일치하도록 빈칸을 채우시오.

> = The TV is _____ heavy that _____ _____ lift it.

20 밑줄 친 ⓑ에 알맞은 단어는?

① to
② can
③ enough
④ that
⑤ too

[01–03] 다음 빈칸에 알맞은 것을 고르시오.

01

> He is _____ drive a car.
> 그는 자동차를 운전할 만큼 충분히 나이가 들었다.

① old enough to
② too old to
③ enough old to
④ old enough
⑤ enough old

02

> He was so sick that he _____ not do homework.
> 그는 너무 아파서 숙제를 할 수가 없었다.

① can
② does
③ did
④ could
⑤ will

03

> This food is too spicy _____ to eat.
> 이 음식은 너무 매워서 외국인들이 먹을 수 없다.

① foreigners
② of foreigners
③ from foreigners
④ for foreigners
⑤ to foreigners

04 다음 빈 칸에 들어가기에 알맞은 것은?

> It is wise of you _____ a gift.
> 네가 선물을 준비한 것은 현명하다.

① preparing
② to preparing
③ to prepare
④ to prepared
⑤ to have prepared

05 다음 문장의 괄호 안에서 알맞은 것에 O표 해보시오.

> This watch is too expensive for me to buy. = This watch is so expensive that I (can, cannot) buy it.

06 다음 빈칸에 of가 들어가기에 올바르지 <u>않은</u> 것은?

① It is rude _____ you to call him at late night.
② It was very careless _____ you to go out late.
③ It was wise _____ you not to fight.
④ It is polite _____ you to help your teacher.
⑤ It is sorry _____ you to lose your job.

07 다음 괄호 안의 말이 들어갈 알맞은 자리를 고르시오.

(for her)
① It is ② not easy ③ to overcome
④ her father's death. ⑤

08 다음 각 빈칸에 들어갈 말이 알맞게 짝지어진 것을 고르시오.

_____ is stupid _____ him not to wear seat belt.

① It - for
② It - of
③ It - to
④ That - for
⑤ That - of

[9-10] 다음 밑줄 친 단어와 바꿔 쓸 수 있는 말을 고르시오.

09

He is not sure what to do.

① for do
② to doing
③ he does
④ he should
⑤ he should do

10

We didn't decide when to meet.

① we meet
② we should meet
③ we should
④ we should decide
⑤ we meet to decide

11 다음 문장을 바르게 영작한 것을 고르시오.

그녀는 마실 따뜻한 것을 원한다.

① She wants to drink warm something.
② She wants something to drink warm.
③ She wants warm something to drink.
④ She wants something warm to drink.
⑤ She wants to drink something warm.

12 다음 ( )안의 말을 우리말에 맞게 배열하시오.

He needs _____ .
(to, someone, lean on)
그는 누군가 기댈 사람이 필요하다.

lean on 기대다

13 다음 ( )안의 단어를 이용하여 우리말에 알맞게 영작하시오.

> 여기에 알아야 할 유용한 모든 것이 있다.
>
> Here is _____.
>
> (know, useful, everything)

[14–15] 다음 글을 읽고 물음에 답하시오.

> Today, my mother went to a supermarket to buy bottles of water. She tried to move them by herself. But they were ⓐ <u>heavy too</u> for her to move. She was so embarrassed that she ⓑ <u>cannot</u> do anything. Then, some students helped her to move the water to her car.
>
> ⓒ _____.
>
> (그들이 나의 엄마를 도운 것은 친절했다.)

14 ⓐ, ⓑ의 어법상 <u>어색한</u> 부분을 바르게 고치시오.

ⓐ heavy too → _____

ⓑ cannot → _____

15 다음 ⓒ의 문장을 바르게 영작한 것을 고르시오.

① It was kind for them to help my mom.

② It was too kind for them to help my mom.

③ It was kind of them to help my mom.

④ It was too kind of them to help my mom.

⑤ It was so kind that my mom helped them.

16 두 문장의 뜻이 같지 <u>않은</u> 것을 고르시오.

① The question is easy enough for him to solve.
  = The question is so easy that he can't solve it.

② Bob is too young to support his parents.
  = Bob is so young that he can't support his parents.

③ Kate is kind enough to guide you.
  = Kate is so kind that she can guide you.

④ He is too excited to sleep.
  = He is so excited that he can't sleep.

⑤ The man was rich enough to buy the car.
  = The man was so rich that he could buy the car.

support 부양하다

17 다음 빈칸에 알맞지 <u>않은</u> 것을 고르시오.

> It is _____ of him to take the class.

① clever
② wise
③ smart
④ foolish
⑤ important

18 우리말에 맞게 괄호 안의 단어를 배열하시오.

> She wants _____.
> (nice, to, something, wear)
>
> 그녀는 입을 멋진 (어떤)것을 원한다.

19 다음에서 밑줄 친 부분을 바르게 고치시오.

> He should prepare <u>things a lot of</u> to cheer up his child.
>
> 그는 그의 아이를 북돋기 위해 많은 것들을 준비해야 한다.

things a lot of → _____

20 두 문장의 뜻이 같도록 빈칸에 알맞은 말을 쓰시오.

> My sister knows how to make spaghetti.
> = My sister knows how _____ _____ make spaghetti.

Chapter 2

부정사 B

UNIT 1

목적보어로 쓰인 명사와 형용사, 부정사

5형식 문장에서는 목적보어로 명사와 형용사, 부정사, 분사(~ing, ~ed)가 올 수 있다. 본 unit에서는 목적보어로 명사와 형용사, 부정사가 오는 경우를 공부해 보자.

🟦 목적보어가 명사일 때

| 주어 | + | make   call
name   elect
consider…. | + | 목적어 | + | 명사 |

ex. I made <u>my son</u> <u>an actor</u>. 나는 나의 아들을 배우로 만들었다.
　　　　 목적어　　목적보어 (명사)　　　(my son = an actor)

🟦 목적격보어가 형용사일 때

| 주어 | + | make   keep
find   leave
think   consider…. | + | 목적어 | + | 형용사 |

ex. She made <u>my mom</u> <u>happy</u>. 그녀는 나의 엄마를 행복하게 만들었다.
　　　　　 목적어　　목적보어(형용사)　　　(my mom = happy)

🔷 목적보어가 부정사일 때

| 주어 | + | want
ask
expect
warn 경고하다
remind 상기시키다. 생각나게하다 | tell
advise
order | + | 목적어 | + | to부정사 |

ex. I <u>want</u> **him** <u>to get</u> a job. 나는 그가 일자리를 얻기를 원한다.
　　주어　동사　목적어　　　목적보어

* 3형식과 5형식

ex. I <u>want</u> to get a job. (3형식) 나는 (내가) 일자리를 얻기를 원한다.
　　주어　동사　　　목적어

ex. I <u>want</u> **him** to get a job. (5형식) 나는 그가 일자리를 얻기를 원한다.
　　주어　동사　목적어　　　목적보어

Tip! 5형식은 3형식인 '주어 + 동사 + 목적어' 뒤에 보어를 붙여준 문장을 말한다. 그래서 5형식 보어를 목적(격)보어라고 한다.
　　　주어 + 동사 + 목적어 + 목적(격)보어

부정사는 그 근본이 동사에 뿌리를 두고 있기 때문에 동사의 성질을 가지고 있다. 따라서 영어의 기본적인 어순인 '주어 + 동사'에 따라 부정사의 주어는 부정사 바로 앞에 온다고 생각하면 된다.
즉, 5형식 문장은 ' 주어1 + 동사1 + 주어2 + 동사2 '라고 생각하면 이해가 쉽다.

ex. I <u>want</u> **you** <u>to leave</u>. 나는 원한다 + 네가 떠나기를
　　주어1 동사1　주어2　　동사2　　　주어1 동사1　주어2 동사2

* hope, decide는 목적보어가 있는 5형식문장을 만들 수 없음에 주의해야 한다.

ex. I hope to be a soldier. 나는 군인이 되기를 희망한다.

~~I hope him to be a soldier.~~ 나는 그가 군인이 되기를 희망한다.

다음 중 목적어와 목적보어를 찾아 ○표 하고, 우리말로 옮겨 보자.

1 We called (him)(Jimmy).

우리는 　　　　그를　　　　 Jimmy라고 　　　불렀다.

2 They considered Spider-Man a hero.

그들은 　　　　　　　　　　　　　여겼다.

3 The news made me sad.

그 소식은 　　　　　　　　　　　만들었다.

4 Mothers all over the world think their children smart.

온 세상의 엄마들은 　　　　　　　　 생각한다.

5 I left the door open.

나는 　　　　　　　　　　　　　두었다.

다음 중 목적어와 목적보어를 찾아 ○표 하고, 우리말로 옮겨 보자.

1 He wants (to go to college). 　　그는 　 대학에 가기를 　 원한다.

　　He wants me to go to college. 　그는 　　　　　　　　 원한다.

2 Tom expected her to leave Paris. 　Tom은 　　　　　　　 기대했다.

　　Tom expected to leave Paris. 　Tom은 　　　 기대했다.

3 She wants to play outside. 　그녀는 　　　　　 원한다.

　　She wants her son to play outside. 　그녀는 　　　　　　　 원한다.

consider 생각하다, 여기다, 숙고하다　　leave 떠나다, (그대로) 두다

다음 중 목적어와 목적보어에 ○표 하고, 우리말에 알맞게 주어진 단어들을 나열해 보자.

1 They _elected_ _Tom_ _captain_ . (Tom, captain, elected)
그들은 (Tom을)(대장으로) 뽑았다.

2 I . (Paul, named, my baby)
나는 나의 아기를 Paul이라고 이름 지었다.

3 She . (slim, her body, kept)
그녀는 그녀의 몸을 날씬하게 유지했다.

4 We . (alive, found, him)
우리는 그가 살아 있는 것을 알아냈다.

5 She . (her husband, "honey", calls)
그녀는 그녀의 남편을 "honey"라고 부른다.

6 He . (made, her, his wife)
그는 그녀를 그의 아내로 삼았다.

7 Jenny . (me, small and weak, considers)
Jenny는 나를 작고 약하다고 여긴다.

8 Tom . (wonderful, her house, found)
Tom은 그녀의 집이 멋지다는 것을 발견했다.

9 I . (think, him, kind and generous)
나는 그가 친절하고 너그럽다고 생각한다.

10 He . (got, his shirt, dirty)
그는 그의 셔츠를 더럽게 했다.

---

elect 뽑다   **name** 이름짓다   **find** 발견하다, 알아내다

다음 중 목적어와 목적보어에 O표 하고, 우리말에 알맞게 주어진 단어를 나열해 보자.

1 They *want us to stay* longer. (us, want, stay, to)

그들은 (우리가) (더 오래 머물기를) 원한다.

2 I _____. (calm down, her, told, to)

나는 그녀에게 진정하라고 말했다.

3 She _____ a warm coat. (advised, to, wear, her son)

그녀는 그녀의 아들에게 따뜻한 코트를 입으라고 충고했다.

4 He _____ for 1 hour. (me, asked, to, wait)

그는 나에게 한 시간을 기다리라고 부탁했다.

5 We _____. (made, her, our role model)

우리는 그녀를 우리의 모범으로 삼았다.

6 She _____ a green onion. (to, me, buy, reminded)

그녀는 나에게 파를 살 것을 상기시켰다.

7 I _____ 'Yes'. (expected, to, say, them)

나는 그들이 '예'라고 대답하기를 기대했다.

8 The general _____ forward. (to, go, them, ordered)

그 장군은 그들에게 전진하라고 명령했다.

9 My dad _____ games. (stay away from, warned, to, me)

나의 아빠는 나에게 게임을 멀리하라고 경고하셨다.

10 My family _____. (doesn't want, dad, retire, to)

나의 가족은 아빠가 은퇴하시길 원치 않는다.

---

calm down 진정하다   **green onion** 파   **stay away from** ~을 멀리하다   **retire** 은퇴하다

다음 중 목적어와 목적보어에 ○표 하고 우리말에 알맞게 문장을 완성해 보자.

1 They elected *him* *president of our class* .

그들은 (그를)(우리반의 반장으로) 뽑았다.

2 He left .

그는 나를 홀로 남겨두었다.

3 He wants healthy.

그는 그의 엄마가 건강하게 유지하기를 원한다.

4 She named .

그녀는 그것에게 "Moomoo"라고 이름을 지어줬다.

5 His friends considered .

그의 친구들은 그를 개그맨으로 여겼다.

6 We found .

우리는 Bill이 매우 게으르다는 것을 알았다.

7 She left .

그녀는 그 강아지를 혼자 놔 두었다.

8 People call .

사람들은 그 시계를 'Big Ben'이라 부른다.

9 Jane expected the truth.

Jane은 그가 진실을 말할 것을 기대했다.

10 It makes .

그것은 그녀를 편안하게 만든다.

---

president of the class 반장   **comedian** 개그맨   **fool** 바보   **puppy** 강아지   **alone** 혼자, 홀로
comfortable 편안한

다음 중 목적어와 목적보어에 O표 하고 주어진 단어를 이용하여 우리말에 알맞게 문장을 완성해 보자.

1 Angela *advised* *him* *to take* a rest. (take)

Angela는 그에게 휴식을 취하라고 충고했다

2 My mom _____ to the academy. (go)

나의 엄마는 내가 그 학원에 갈 것을 요구했다.

3 She doesn't _____ an old suit. (wear)

그녀는 그녀의 남편이 낡은 정장 입기를 원하지 않는다.

4 She _____ the leg of the table. (fix)

그녀는 Tom에게 탁자의 다리를 고칠 것을 상기시켰다.

5 His uncle _____ the door. (shut)

그의 삼촌은 그녀에게 문을 닫으라고 말했다.

6 The teacher _____ on time. (be)

선생님은 우리에게 제시간에 오라고 경고했다.

7 Andy _____ the competition. (win)

Andy는 그의 딸이 그 대회에서 이기기를 원했다.

8 The professor _____ him. (follow)

그 교수는 조수에게 그를 따라오라고 명령했다.

9 My dad _____ my boyfriend. (break up with)

나의 아빠는 나에게 나의 남자 친구와 헤어지라고 충고했다.

10 The king _____ the lion. (kill)

그 왕은 John에게 그 사자를 죽이라고 명령했다.

---

academy 학원   warn 경고하다   competition 경쟁, 대회   assistant 조수
break up with ~와 결별하다, 헤어지다

다음 문장이 어법상 옳으면 ○표 틀리면 ×표 하자.

1   She wanted me to pass the exam.   ○

2   His father hoped him to be an artist.

3   They expected us to be diligent.

4   I hoped to attend the meeting.

5   My parents decided me to go abroad for study.

6   He hopes her to be a celebrity.

7   Jane decided to stay in London.

8   My mother told me to hold an umbrella.

9   They hope their boss to accept it.

10 He asked her to wash his clothes.

11 Tom decided me to end it all.

12 Karl advised us to come early.

13 She hopes her daughter to be rich.

14 We want you to be safe.

15 Bob decided Judy to leave for a business trip to China.

---

abroad 해외로   leave for a business trip 출장가다

UNIT 2

목적보어로 쓰인 원형부정사

원형 부정사란?

to가 없는 부정사를 말하며, 5형식 문장에서 동사에 따라 원형부정사나 to부정사를 써야 한다.

---

1 5형식에서 목적보어로 쓰인 원형 부정사

🔹 **지각동사 : 감각** (보다, 듣다, 느끼다...)을 나타내는 동사

| 주어 | + | see, watch, look at
hear, listen to
feel ... | + | 목적어 | + | 원형부정사 |

ex. I **saw** him **enter** the house. 나는 그가 집에 들어가는 것을 보았다.

🔹 **사역동사 : 남에게 무엇인가 하도록 시키는 동사**

| 주어 | + | make 시키다 / 만들다 (강요)
have 시키다 / 하게 하다 (부탁)
let 허락하다 / 내버려두다 | + | 목적어 | + | 원형부정사 |

ex. I **had** him **do** his homework. 나는 그에게 숙제하도록 시켰다.

| 주어 | + | get 시키다/하게 하다 | + | 목적어 | + | to부정사 |

ex. I **got** him **to sign** on the paper. 나는 그가 그 서류에 서명하게 했다.

| 주어 | + | help ~하는 것을 도와주다 | + | 목적어 | + | 원형부정사
to부정사 |

ex. I **helped** him **(to) do** the work. 나는 그가 그 일을 하는 것을 도와주었다.

다음 주어진 문장을 우리말로 옮겨 보자.

1 Mom had her son clean the house.

엄마는 　　　　　　　　*그녀의 아들에게 집을 청소하게 시켰다*　　　　　　　.

Mom had dinner with her friend.

엄마는 　　　　　　　　*그녀의 친구와 저녁을 먹었다*　　　　　　　.

2 The teacher made us memorize 300 new words.

선생님은 　　　　　　　　　　　　　　　　　　.

The teacher made out students' records.

선생님은 　　　　　　　　　　　　　　　　　　.

3 She got a lot of information.

그녀는 　　　　　　　　　　　　　　　　　　.

She got her son to bring his friends.

그녀는 　　　　　　　　　　　　　　　　　　.

4 They let me go there.

그들은 　　　　　　　　　　　　　　　　　　.

Let's do it.

우리 　　　　　　　　　　　　　　　　　　.

5 He helped the old man (to) carry the package.

그는 　　　　　　　　　　　　　　　　　　.

He helped the old man.

그는 　　　　　　　　　　　　　　　　　　.

memorize 암기하다, 외우다　　**word** 단어　　**information** 정보　　**bring** 가져오다, 데려오다
package 짐꾸러미　　**make out** 만들다, 작성하다　　**students' records** 성적표

보기에서 알맞은 것을 골라 써 넣어 보자.

| 보기 |

get	watch	order	let	feel
want	make	tell	help	ask
remind	see	look at	allow	hear
advise	expect	have	listen to	

〈일반동사〉

1 주어 _order_ + 목적어 + to부정사

〈지각동사〉   〈사역동사〉

2 주어 + 목적어 + 원형부정사

—

—

—

〈사역동사〉

3 주어 + 목적어 + to부정사

〈사역동사〉

4 주어 + 목적어 + to부정사 / 원형부정사

allow 허락하다

다음 중 동사에 O표를 하고, 알맞은 것을 골라 보자. (두 개 가능)

1 He ⟨advises⟩ me (learn, ⟨to learn⟩) Chinese.

2 She saw a bird (fly, to fly) over the tree.

3 I hope (be, to be) a singer in the future.

4 We heard her (come, to come) in the room.

5 Kate asked him (play, to play) the cello.

6 They felt the wind (blow, to blow) hard.

7 The father let his daughter (to sleep, sleep).

8 My teacher wanted us (draw, to draw) the flowers.

9 Mr. Kim got his daughter (to cook, cook) rice.

10 He watched a dog (run, to run) fast.

11 She listened to him (speak, to speak) to himself.

12 I had him (wash, to wash) my car.

13 Peter helped her (to wrap, wrap) the gift.

14 Her mom made her (do, to do) her homework.

15 He let the dragonfly (fly, to fly) into the sky.

다음 중 동사에 O표를 하고, 알맞은 것을 골라 보자. (두 개 가능)

1 My mom (let) me ((play), to play) with the puppy.

2 We wanted them (come, to come) back to Korea.

3 The gift made her (feel, to feel) happy.

4 Jim ordered her (do, to do) it herself.

5 She watched us (build, to build) a tent.

6 Did Nancy let him (stay, to stay) home yesterday?

7 Adam saw a lion (sleep, to sleep) under the big tree.

8 It made her (change, to change) her mind.

9 We heard a cat (catch, to catch) a small mouse.

10 Sally asked him (leave, to leave) here as soon as possible.

11 Brian doesn't help her (water, to water) the roses.

12 Dad made me (get, to get) a good grade.

13 My mom expects me (take, to take) care of my little brother.

14 He ordered me (be, to be) more careful.

15 She felt something (crawl, to crawl) on her hand.

as soon as possible 가능한   **crawl** 기어가다

다음 중 동사에 ○표 하고, 주어진 단어를 알맞은 형태로 바꿔 써 넣어 보자.

1 She (helps) me   *(to) work*   every day. (work)

2 The boss felt her   a break time. (need)

3 He had her   his car. (clean)

4 He made her   some tea. (prepare)

5 She told him   his teacher. (meet)

6 He advised me   there on time. (get)

7 You should have him   at 6 a.m. (get up)

8 He got his son   the chair. (paint)

9 I heard the man   Jack the way to the station. (show)

10 We saw the fire fighters   the fire. (put out)

---

put out (불을) 끄다   **fire** 불

다음 주어진 단어를 이용하여 우리말에 알맞게 문장을 완성해 보자. (부정사 사용)

1 I ___saw___ ___him___ ___enter___ the house. (see, enter)

나는 그가 그 집으로 들어가는 것을 보았다.

2 Mom _____ till 12 o'clock. (tell, study)

엄마는 나에게 12시까지 공부하라고 말했다.

3 We _____ us. (feel, look at)

우리는 그녀가 우리를 쳐다보고 있는 것을 느꼈다.

4 Mary _____ in the room. (hear, snore)

Mary는 그가 방에서 코고는 것을 들었다.

5 Jack _____ the car. (help, park)

Jack은 내가 차를 주차하는 것을 도와주었다.

6 She _____ nothing. (let, do)

그녀는 그녀의 아들이 아무것도 하지 못하게 한다.

7 He _____ 20 sentences. (make, write)

그는 우리에게 20개 문장을 쓰도록 시켰다.

8 I _____ Bill. (allow, marry)

나는 나의 딸이 Bill과 결혼하는 것을 허락했다.

9 Dad _____ healthy. (want, be)

아빠는 그의 아들이 건강하기를 바라신다.

10 _____ there. (let, go)

그들이 거기에 가게 내버려둬라.

---

snore 코를 골다

D 기본 TEST

정답 및 해설 p.7

다음 주어진 단어를 이용하여 우리말에 알맞게 문장을 완성해 보자. (부정사 사용)

1 She *had* *her son* *do* his homework. (do, have)

그녀는 그녀의 아들이 숙제를 하도록 시켰다.

2 Joe _____ down. (fall, watch)

Joe는 그 잎들이 떨어지는 것을 보았다.

3 Dad _____ camping with my friends. (go, allow)

아빠는 내가 친구들과 캠핑가는 것을 허락했다.

4 She _____ the dishes. (help, wash)

그녀는 그녀의 엄마가 설거지하는 것을 돕는다.

5 My mom _____ TV. (watch, let)

나의 엄마는 내가 TV를 보도록 내버려 두셨다.

6 The teacher _____ a jump rope. (bring, tell)

선생님은 우리에게 줄넘기를 가져오라고 말했다.

7 Adam _____ close. (feel, come)

Adam은 한 낯선 사람이 가까이 오는 것을 느꼈다.

8 His speech _____ her mind. (change, make)

그의 연설은 그녀가 그녀의 마음을 바꾸도록 만들었다.

9 He _____ with a ball indoors. (play, let)

그는 우리가 실내에서 공놀이를 하도록 내버려 두었다.

10 Paul _____ out of the house. (get, hear)

Paul은 그녀가 집 밖으로 나가는 것(소리)을 들었다.

---

jump rope 줄넘기   sentence 문장   indoors 실내에서   get out of ~에서 나가다

UNIT 3

지각동사＋목적어＋현재분사 (~ing)
have＋목적어＋원형 부정사/과거분사 (~ed)
get＋목적어＋to 부정사/과거분사 (~ed)

◆ 지각동사 + 목적어 + 현재분사 (~ing)

목적어가 동작을 하는 순간을 지각하는 것을 말한다.

ex. I saw him **entering** the house. 나는 그가 집에 들어가고 있는 것을 (순간을) 보았다.

◆ have + 목적어 + 원형 부정사 / 과거분사 (~ed)
　 get + 목적어 + to 부정사 / 과거분사 (~ed)

have get	+ 목적어 +	원형 부정사 to 부정사	~시키다, ~하게 하다

목적어와 목적보어의 관계가 능동이면, have는 원형부정사, get은 to부정사를 쓴다.

ex. I **had** him **fix** my computer. 나는 그에게 내 컴퓨터를 고치게 했다.
　　 I **got** him **to fix** my computer.

* 목적어인 그가 목적보어인 내 컴퓨터를 고치므로 능동관계이다.

have get	+ 목적어 +	과거분사 (~ed)	① ~시키다, ~하게 하다 (주어가 시킨 일) ② ~당하다 (주어가 시키지 않은 일)

목적어와 목적보어의 관계가 수동이면, 모두 과거분사를 쓴다.

ex 1. I **had(got)** my computer **fixed**. 나는 내 컴퓨터를 고치도록 시켰다.
ex 2. I **had(got)** my purse **stolen**. 나는 내 지갑을 도둑질 당했다. (도둑맞았다).

* 목적어인 나의 컴퓨터가 목적보어인 고침을 당하므로 수동관계이다.

Tip! 주어가 시키지 않은 일은 '당하다'로 해석한다.

목적어와 목적보어에 ○표 하고, 우리말로 옮겨 보자.

1 He saw ⟨her⟩ ⟨eating something at night .⟩

→ 그는 　　　　　*그녀가*　　　　　*밤에 무언가를 먹는 것을*　　　　　보았다.

2 We heard him sneezing in the bathroom.

→ 우리는 　　　　　　　　　　　　　　　　들었다.

3 Look at the spider coming down from the ceiling.

→ 　　　　　　　　　　　　　　　　처다봐라.

4 They watched the sky turning red.

→ 그들은 　　　　　　　　　　　　　　지켜보았다.

5 She heard a bird chirping in the backyard.

→ 그녀는 　　　　　　　　　　　　　　들었다.

목적어와 목적보어에 ○표 하고, 우리말로 옮겨 보자.

1 He got ⟨his shoes⟩ ⟨mended.⟩

그는 　　　　　*그의 신발을 수선시켰다*　　　　　.

He got John to mend his shoes.

그는 　　　　　　　　　　　　　　　.

2 Jane had her hair dyed.

Jane은 　　　　　　　　　　　　　　.

Jane had the hairdresser dye her hair.

Jane은 　　　　　　　　　　　　　　.

---

sneeze 재채기하다　　**ceiling** 천장　　**chirp** 지저귀다　　**mend** 수선하다　　**dye** 염색하다

A 기본 TEST

다음 중 알맞은 것을 골라 보자.

1 Mom had me (turn, turned, to turn) on the fan.
엄마는 나에게 선풍기를 켜라고 시켰다.

2 Dad had the car (wash, washed, to wash) yesterday.
아빠는 어제 차를 세차시켰다.

3 I had my purse (steal, stealing, stolen) in the subway.
나는 지하철 안에서 내 지갑을 도난당했다.

4 My brother had his homework (check, checked, to check) by the teacher.
내 남동생은 선생님에게 그의 숙제를 검사 받았다.

5 He got James (paint, painted, to paint) the four walls.
그는 James가 사방의 벽을 칠하게 시켰다.

6 She got the stairs (repair, repaired, to repair) by me.
그녀는 나에게 계단을 수리하도록 했다. (계단이 나에 의해서 수리되도록 했다)

7 My uncle has his shoes (polish, polished, to polish) every day.
나의 삼촌은 매일 그의 구두를 광이 나게 한다.

8 The president had his staffs (promote, promoted, to promote).
대통령은 그의 참모들을 승진시켰다.

9 She got the bed (remove, removed, to remove) out of the room.
그녀는 그 침대를 방 밖으로 치웠다. (그 침대가 방밖으로 치워지게 시켰다)

10 My sister had her hair (wave, waved, to wave) .
나의 여동생은 그녀의 머리에 웨이브를 넣었다.

---

staff 직원, 참모   promote 승진시키다   remove 치우다

다음 주어진 단어를 이용하여 우리말에 알맞게 문장을 완성해 보자. (두 개 가능)

1 We _heard_ _her_ _singing/sing_ . (hear, sing)

우리는 그녀가 노래 부르는 것을 들었다.

2 I . (see, dance)

나는 그들이 춤추는 것을 보았다.

3 Tom off. (feel, start)

Tom은 버스가 출발하는 것을 느꼈다.

4 My sister . (get, pierce)

내 누나는 그녀의 귀를 뚫도록 했다.

5 She didn't . (hear, pop)

그녀는 풍선이 터지는 것을 듣지 못했다.

6 They . (look at, set)

그들은 해가 지는 것을 바라보았다.

7 Dad . (have, iron)

아빠는 그의 셔츠를 다리게 시켰다.

8 People . (have, punish)

사람들이 그 남자를 처벌받게 했다.

9 Mom the oven. (get, turn off)

엄마는 나에게 오븐을 끄게 시켰다.

10 I . (have, cut)

나는 나의 머리를 자르도록 했다.

---

set (해가) 지다   pierce 뚫다   ballon 풍선   pop 뻥하고 터지다   iron 다림질하다   punish 벌 주다

4

부정사의 부정, 관용적으로 쓰이는 부정사, 독립부정사

● 부정사의 부정은 부정사 앞에 not, never만 붙이면 된다.

ex. I want my daughter **not to be** a doctor. 나는 나의 딸이 의사가 되지 않기를 바란다.

● 관용적으로 쓰이는 원형 부정사

아래의 경우 관용적으로 뒤에 원형 부정사를 사용한다.

had better ~하는 편이 낫다

cannot but ~하지 않을 수 없다

do nothing but ~하기만 한다   +   원형부정사

may well ~하는 것은 당연하다

may as well ~하는 게 좋겠다

ex. He **cannot but** believe her. 그는 그녀를 믿지 않을 수 없다.

Tip! cannot but이나 do nothing but에서 but은 '~외에'라는 뜻을 가진다. 그러므로 직역을 하면 외우기 쉽다.
cannot but은 '~외에는 할 수 없다 (~하지 않을 수 없다)', do nothing but은 '~외에는 아무것도 하지 않는다 (~하기만 한다)'
로 이해해 보자.

● 독립부정사

주로 문장 앞에서 독립적으로 사용되면서 문장 전체를 꾸며준다.

to tell the truth	사실을 말하자면
to be honest	정직하게 말하자면
to be frank with you	솔직히 말해서
to make matters worse	설상가상으로
strange to say	이상한 이야기지만
so to speak	소위, 말하자면
not to mention ~	~은 말할 것도 없이

ex. **To be honest** with you, it is so complex. 너에게 정직하게 말하자면, 그건 너무 복잡해.

주어진 단어를 이용하여 부정사의 부정을 만들고 우리말로 옮겨 보자.

1 Bill expected her to go there. (not)

Bill expected *her* *not to go there* .

→ Bill은 *그녀가* *거기에 가지 않기를* 기대했다.

2 Dad advised me to get up late. (not)

Dad advised .

→ 아빠는 충고했다.

3 She told us to cross at the red light. (never)

She told .

→ 그녀는 말했다.

4 He warned her to open the box. (never)

He warned .

→ 그는 경고했다.

다음 중 알맞은 것을 골라 보자.

1 Mom told (her not to climb , not climb to her) up the tree.

2 She advised (us not to swim, us to not swim) in the river.

3 I wanted (the baby to not touch, the baby not to touch) my things.

4 He reminded (burn not to her, her not to burn) the meat.

5 Lisa asked (never to tell me, me never to tell) the secret to others.

at the red light 빨간불에   burn 태우다   secret 비밀   others 다른 사람들

다음 중 보기에서 알맞은 것을 골라 연결해 보자.

| 보기 |

A. had better
B. cannot but
C. may as well
D. may well
E. do nothing but

a. ~하는 것은 당연하다
b. ~하는 게 좋겠다
c. ~하는 편이 낫다
d. ~하기만 한다
e. ~하지 않을 수 없다

1 A – C , B – , C – , D – , E – .

| 보기 |

A. to tell the truth
B. to be honest
C. to be frank with you
D. to make matters worse
E. strange to say
F. so to speak
G. not to mention ~

a. 사실을 말하자면
b. 정직하게 말하자면
c. 소위, 말하자면
d. 설상가상으로
e. 이상한 이야기지만
f. ~은 말할 것도 없이
g. 솔직히 말해서

2 A – , B – , C – , D – , E – ,

F – , G – .

다음 중 알맞은 것을 골라 보자.

1 He worked harder (to get, get) a promotion.

2 The woman had better (to find, find) some shelter.

3 She doesn't like (to study, study) English.

4 Kate may well (to act, act) like that.

5 He did nothing but (to jog, jog) all the time.

6 We cannot but (to keep, keep) the traffic rule.

7 Susan saw the bees (to fly, fly) among the flowers.

8 I want (to ask, ask) you something.

9 He ran into the church (to hide, hide) himself.

10 Mark woke up early (to exercise, exercise) at the gym.

11 You may as well (to change, change) your shirt.

12 Erica is happy (to see, see) her old friend.

13 Mom got me (to mince, mince) the pork.

14 The soldiers cannot but (to obey, obey) the general's order.

15 She may well (to be, be, being) tired after the hard-working.

promotion 승진   shelter 안식처   traffic rule 교통 법규   mince 다지다   general 장군   obey 복종하다

A 기본 TEST

주어진 단어를 알맞은 형태로 바꿔 넣어 보자.

1 He walked to the mall *to return* the coat. (return)

2 She cannot but   at the sight. (laugh)

3 He promised me   that. (do)

4 You may well   so. (say)

5 We may as well   it. (do)

6 James will go to Internet cafe   for his son. (look)

7 I heard someone   through the window. (come)

8 Maybe we had better   working right now. (start)

9 All our relatives came to my house   dinner together. (eat)

10 Bears do nothing but   in winter. (sleep)

Internet cafe PC방   relatives 친척

주어진 단어를 이용하여 우리말에 알맞게 영어로 완성해 보자.

1 Jim said to me *not to tell* it to anyone. (tell)

Jim이 나에게 그것을 아무에게도 말하지 말라고 말했다.

2 We a taxi. (take)

우리는 택시를 타는 편이 낫겠어.

3 She TV every weekend. (watch)

그녀는 매 주말 텔레비전을 보기만 한다.

4 He warned us Saudi Arabia because of MERS. (visit)

그는 우리에게 메르스때문에 사우디아라비아를 방문하지 말라고 경고했다.

5 My dad promised mom . (drink)

나의 아빠는 엄마에게 결코 술을 마시지 않겠다고 약속했다.

6 I tried our departure. (delay)

나는 우리의 출발을 지연시키지 않으려고 노력했다.

7 You a dentist. (see)

너는 치과에 가는 게 좋겠다.

8 Mr. Bush proud of his daughter. (be)

Bush씨가 그의 딸을 자랑스러워하는 것은 당연하다.

9 They with his opinion. (agree)

그들은 그의 의견에 동의하지 않을 수 없다.

10 We have to wash our hands a cold. (catch)

우리는 감기에 걸리지 않기 위해서 우리의 손을 씻어야만 한다.

---

departure 출발 **agree** 동의하다 **Saudi Arabia** 사우디아라비아 **MERS** 메르스 **drink** 술을 마시다
delay 지연하다

우리말에 알맞게 문장을 완성해 보자.

1 _To be frank with you_ , I met him yesterday.

솔직히 말해서, 나는 어제 그를 만났어.

2 I'm going to   next week.

나는 다음 주에 쉬기만 하려고 한다.

3 We   with his suggestion.

우리는 그의 제안에 동의하지 않을 수 없다.

4   , only she didn't know the rumor.

이상한 이야기지만, 그녀만 그 소문을 몰랐다.

5 I don't really care,   .

정직하게 말하자면, 나는 정말 관심이 없다.

6 You   in English.

너는 영어로 말하는 것이 낫겠다.

7 I   her later.

나는 나중에 그녀에게 전화하는게 좋겠다.

8   , I'm not close to him.

사실을 말하자면, 나는 그와 가깝게 지내지 않아.

9 He   so.

그가 그렇게 말하는 것은 당연하다.

10 I am his guardian,   .

말하자면, 내가 그의 후견인이다.

---

suggestion 제안   **rumor** 소문   **close** 가까운   **guardian** 후견인

01 우리말을 영어로 바르게 옮긴 것을 고르시오.

> 엄마는 내가 더 열심히 공부하기를 원한다.

① Mom wants me to study harder.
② Mom wants to study me harder.
③ Mom wants me study harder.
④ Mom wants to me study harder.
⑤ Mom wants harder to study me.

02 다음 문장에서 우리말과 일치하도록 not이 들어가야 하는 위치는?

> James는 나에게 이 호수에서 수영하지 말라고 말했다.
> → James ① told ② me ③ to ④ swim ⑤ in this lake.

03 다음 중 올바르지 않은 문장을 고르시오.

① Danny saw her eat an apple.
② I had her clean the room.
③ She helped me do that.
④ I heard him to say like that.
⑤ Mary looked at me enter the gate.

04 다음 빈칸에 알맞은 것을 고르시오.

> My dad _____ me to play baseball over there.

① told
② let
③ had
④ made
⑤ saw

05 다음 대화의 내용에 맞게 문장을 완성하시오.

> *Christie* : How about going to the gym?
> *Tommy* : No, I don't think that's a good idea. We have an exam tomorrow.
> *Christie* : Okay, let's go to the library.

→ Christie and Tommy decided _____ to go to the gym.

How about ~ing..? ~하는 게 어때?

[06–07] ( ) 안에서 알맞은 것을 고르시오.

06 Mike helped her (to clean, cleaning) the kitchen.

07 I saw the boy (steal, to steal) the bicycle.

08 다음 중 어법상 알맞지 <u>않은</u> 것은?

① George helped her to get the job.
② The pictures helped me read this book.
③ Raining helps the city being cleaning.
④ My mother helped me make some cookies.
⑤ Exercise helps us to get healthy.

09 다음 중 어법상 알맞은 것은?

① I hope being a nurse.
② Mary advised me go to school early.
③ He had her to go to market.
④ Tom asked her dance.
⑤ She made James tidy up the desk.

tidy up 깔끔하게 정리하다

10 다음 빈칸에 들어갈 수 <u>없는</u> 것을 고르시오.

Joseph _____ me to mow the lawn.

① told
② asked
③ helped
④ got
⑤ had

mow the lawn 잔디를 깎다 ask 요청하다, 물어보다

11 다음 빈칸에 알맞은 말을 고르시오. (두 개)

> 나는 새 한 마리가 날아가는 것을 보았다.
> I saw a bird _____ .

① flies
② is flying
③ flying
④ fly
⑤ to fly

12 다음 중 밑줄 친 것들 중에서 틀린 것을 바르게 고쳐 보자.

> My mom <u>let</u> me <u>to eat</u> anything
> I <u>wanted</u> to eat.

_____ → _____

13 다음 중 바르지 않은 문장 두 개를 고르시오.

① She decided him to go abroad.
② I hope to see you.
③ Christie decided to do it.
④ He hopes her to be a teacher.
⑤ Mary decided to eat dinner with us.

14 다음 빈칸에 들어갈 수 없는 것은?

> My father _____ me water the
> garden.

① let
② got
③ made
④ helped
⑤ had

15 밑줄 친 곳 중에서 잘못된 부분을 찾아 바르게 고치시오.

> 나의 친구는 내가 L.A로 이사가지 않기를 원했다.
> My friend <u>wanted me</u> <u>to not</u>
> <u>move</u> to L.A.

_____ → _____

16 다음 문장에서 never가 놓일 곳을 고르시오.

> ① Jane told ② him ③ to ④ tell
> ⑤ a lie.

[17–18] 다음 빈칸에 알맞은 말을 고르시오.

17

> Jane wants to get her hair _____ .
>
> Jane은 그녀의 머리카락을 파마하기(파마 시키기)를 원한다.

① be permed
② is perm
③ permed
④ perming
⑤ to perm

perm 파마를 하다

18

> My mother had her clock _____ .
>
> 나의 엄마는 그녀의 시계를 수리시켰다.

① repair
② repaired
③ repairing
④ to repair
⑤ did repair

19 다음 빈칸에 들어갈 수 있는 것을 모두 고르시오.

> Tom heard her _____ .

① to sing
② sing
③ sang
④ is singing
⑤ singing

20 다음 문장에서 어색한 부분을 찾아 고치시오.

> Andy had his backpack stealing.
>
> Andy는 그의 가방을 도난당했다.

_____ → _____

steal 훔치다 (stole – stolen)

01 다음 중 어색한 문장을 고르시오.

① He made us happy.
② The movie made me sad.
③ Her parents made her a lawyer.
④ I made him to open the window.
⑤ She made them some cookies.

02 다음 중 빈칸에 to가 들어가지 않는 문장을 고르시오.

① He warned me ____ be careful.
② She advised me ____ study English.
③ Amy had me ____ make lunch.
④ Tom told me ____ be diligent.
⑤ He asked me ____ bring food.

03 다음 독립부정사와 그 의미가 바르게 연결되지 않은 것을 고르시오.

① to tell the truth - 사실을 말하자면
② to be honest - 정직하게 말하자면
③ to be frank with you - 너에게는 미안하지만
④ so to speak - 말하자면, 소위
⑤ not to mention ~ - ~은 말할 것도 없이

04 다음 중 맞는 표현에 O표하시오.

My parents expect me
(be / to be) a diplomat.

diplomat 외교관

05 다음 문장을 우리말로 바르게 옮긴 것은?

I want him to come back.

① 나는 그와 함께 돌아가고 싶다.
② 내가 떠나기를 그는 원한다.
③ 나는 그가 떠나길 원한다.
④ 나는 그에게로 돌아가고 싶다.
⑤ 나는 그가 돌아오길 원한다.

06 다음 문장에서 밑줄 친 부분을 바르게 고치시오.

> I had my bike fix.
> 나는 내 자전거를 수리시켰다.

fix → _____

07 다음 빈칸에 to가 올 수 있는 문장을 고르시오.

① He helped me ____ finish homework.
② I let him ____ do my job.
③ I had my brother ____ wash the dishes.
④ He saw the thief ____ run away.
⑤ She heard me ____ sing.

08 다음 ( )안의 단어를 사용하여 문장을 영작하시오.

> Mom _____ outside.
> (let, play)
> 엄마는 우리가 밖에서 놀도록 내버려두었다.

09 다음 중 밑줄 친 부분이 틀린 문장을 고르시오.

① She got me to listen to her.
② I had him to read my book.
③ He told me to be quiet.
④ We let you go.
⑤ She looked at me take photos.

10 다음 두 문장의 뜻이 같도록 ( )안의 단어를 사용하여 빈칸을 바르게 채워보시오.

> He had her play the piano.
> 그는 그녀에게 피아노를 연주하게 했다.
> = He _____ her _____ the piano.
> (get, play)

11 다음 주어진 단어를 문맥에 맞게 고쳐보시오.

> We had our money _____.
> (steal) 우리는 우리의 돈을 도둑맞았다.

12 다음 중 괄호 안의 단어가 들어갈 알맞은 위치를 고르시오.

> (not)
> My parents ① wish ② me ③ to ④ be ⑤ a singer.
> 나의 부모님은 내가 가수가 되지 않기를 바라신다.

13 다음 중 밑줄 친 부분이 어색한 보기를 고르시오.

① You had better <u>stop</u> eating.
② He cannot but <u>believe</u> her.
③ I turned on my computer <u>to play</u> games.
④ She may well <u>to be</u> angry.
⑤ You may as well <u>take</u> some sleep.

[14-15] 다음 글을 읽고 물음에 답하시오.

> *Diana* : I have a secret to tell you. Will you keep the secret for me?
> *Eva* : Of course, *Diana*.
> *Diana* : To be honest, I like *Tom*.
> *Eva* : Wow, it's amazing!
> *Diana* : Tom is so kind and smart.
> I ⓐ _____ fall in love with him.
> (나는 톰과 사랑에 빠지지 않을 수가 없어.)
> *Eva* : That's sweet. You should tell Tom how you feel about him.
> *Diana* : No, I may as well wait.

14 다음 글의 내용과 일치하는 것을 고르시오.

① Eva와 Diana는 둘 다 Tom을 좋아한다.
② Diana는 Tom에게 마음을 고백할 것이다.
③ Eva는 Diana의 비밀을 지키지 않을 것이다.
④ Diana는 고백을 하지 않고, 기다릴 것이다.
⑤ Eva는 Diana가 고백을 하지 않는 것이 좋다고 생각한다.

15 다음 빈칸에 들어갈 알맞은 원형부정사를 고르시오.

① had better
② cannot but
③ do nothing but
④ may well
⑤ may as well

16 다음 중 빈칸에 to가 필요한 문장을 고르시오.

① We told her ____ watch out.
② A teacher calls me ____ Mr. Kim.
③ I named my dog ____ Happy.
④ He found her ____ alone and sad.
⑤ She made him ____ clean his room.

watch out 조심하다

17 다음 중 목적보어가 있는 5형식 문장을 만들 수 <u>없는</u> 것을 모두 고르시오. (2개)

① I hope you to succeed.
② I want you to succeed.
③ I expect you to succeed.
④ I told him to be diligent.
⑤ I decided him to stay here.

18 다음 빈칸에 to 가 올 수 있는 문장을 고르시오.

① I heard him ＿＿ snore on the sofa.
② He saw her ＿＿ play the violin.
③ She watched them ＿＿ dance.
④ Dad helped me ＿＿ write the essay.
⑤ Mom let me ＿＿ take some rest.

19 다음 중 각각 맞는 표현에 O표 하시오.

· I saw him (called / calling) his father.
　나는 그가 그의 아버지에게 전화를 거는 것을 (순간을) 보았다.

· He had his car (wash / washed) yesterday.
　그는 어제 그의 차를 세차시켰다.

---

20 다음 대화의 빈칸에 들어갈 알맞은 말을 고르시오.

A : You look bad.
B : I didn't sleep well last night. ＿＿＿＿＿＿＿＿ , I have a stomachache.

---

① so to speak
② to be frank with you
③ to tell the truth
④ strange to say
⑤ to make matters worse

Chapter 3

동명사

동명사란?

● 동명사의 역할

동사의 성질을 가지면서 명사의 역할을 하는 것을 말하며, 문장에서 명사가 사용되는 경우에 쓰일 수 있으므로 문장에서 주어, 목적어, 보어로 쓰인다.

ex. **I like skating.** 나는 스케이트 타는 것을 좋아한다.

● 동명사는 부정사와 바꾸어 쓸 수 있다.

ex. **He loves playing soccer.** 그는 축구하는 것을 무척 좋아한다.

= He loves to play soccer.

● 부정사나 동명사를 목적어로 취하는 동사

ⓐ 부정사만을 목적어로 갖는 동사

want, ask, need, hope, plan, expect, decide, wish, promise, would like

ex. **I want to be a scientist.** 나는 과학자가 되기를 원한다. (아직은 과학자가 아님)

ⓑ 동명사만을 목적어로 갖는 동사

mind, enjoy, avoid, give up, keep, spend, finish, practice, deny, dislike, admit, stop, regret

ex. **I enjoy surfing in summer.** 나는 여름에 서핑을 즐긴다. (이미 즐기고 있음)

ⓒ 부정사와 동명사 모두를 목적어로 취할 수 있는 동사

love, hate, like, continue, begin, start

ex. **I like to swim.** 나는 수영하는 것을 좋아한다.

I like swimming. 나는 수영하는 것을 좋아한다.

UNIT 1

목적어(동명사, 부정사)에 따라 뜻이 달라지는 동사

◆ 동명사와 부정사를 취함으로서 의미의 차이를 가지는 동사

ⓐ remember, forget, try는 동명사와 부정사 둘 다를 목적어로 취할 수 있지만 각각 그 의미가 달라진다.

remember	+ ~ing	~한 것을 기억하다
	+ to부정사	~해야 하는 것을 기억하다
forget	+ ~ing	~한 것을 잊다
	+ to부정사	~해야 하는 것을 잊다
try	+ ~ing	(시험 삼아) ~해보다
	+ to부정사	~하려고 노력하다 (시도하다)

ex. He **remembers** go**ing** to the party. 그는 파티에 갔던 것을 기억한다. (이미 파티에 갔다 왔다)
He **remembers to** go to the party. 그는 파티에 갈 것을 기억한다. (아직 파티에 가지 않았다)

ex. He **forgot** meet**ing** Jane. 그는 제인을 만났다는 것을 잊어버렸다. (이미 만났다)
He **forgot to** meet Jane. 그는 제인을 만날 것을 잊어버렸다. (아직 만나지 않았다)

ex. He **tried** mak**ing** a chair. 그는 의자를 (시험삼아) 만들어 보았다. (이미 의자를 만들었음)
He **tried to** make a chair. 그는 의자를 만들려고 노력했다. (아직 의자를 만들지 못했음)

*~ing는 이미 한 것을, to~는 아직 하지 않은 것을 의미한다.

ⓑ stop은 원래 동명사를 목적어로 취하는 동사이나, 뒤에 to부정사가 오는 경우는 부정사의 부사적 용법에 해당되어 '~하기 위해서'라는 뜻을 지닌다.

stop	+ ~ing	~하는 것을 멈추다
	+ to부정사	~하기 위해서 멈추다

ex. He **stopped** smok**ing**. 그는 담배 피우는 것을 멈췄다. (이미 피우고 있었음.)
He **stopped to** smoke. 그는 담배 피우기 위해서 멈췄다. (아직 피우지 않았음.)

Tip! **stop smoking**과 **quit smoking**의 차이
ex. stop smoking을 금연으로 사용하기도 하나 원래는 stop smoking은 담배 피우는 동작을 멈추었다는 것이고, quit smoking은 금연했다는 것으로 그 뜻에 차이가 있다.

다음 주어진 문장을 우리말로 옮겨 보자.

1 Jenny forgot to read the essay.

Jenny는 *그 에세이를 읽어야 하는 것을* 잊어버렸다.

Jenny forgot reading the essay.

Jenny는 잊어버렸다.

2 He stopped to work.

그는 멈추었다.

He stopped working.

그는 멈추었다.

3 We tried to remove it.

우리는 그것을 .

We tried removing it.

우리는 그것을 .

4 The old woman remembers calling on the queen.

그 나이든 여자는 여왕을 기억하고 있다.

The old woman remembers to call on the queen.

그 나이든 여자는 여왕을 기억하고 있다.

---

remove 치우다, 제거하다   **call on** 방문하다

다음 중 알맞은 것을 골라 보자.

1 I forgot (to close, closing) the window.
나는 창문 닫는 것(닫아야 한다는 것)을 잊었다.

2 He remembers (to drop, dropping) by her office.
그는 그녀의 사무실을 들른 것을 기억하고 있다.

3 She forgot (to pull out, pulling out) the plug.
그녀는 코드를 뺀다는 것을 잊어버렸다.

4 He remembers (to meet, meeting) us today.
그는 오늘 우리를 만날 것을 기억하고 있다.

5 Judy stopped (to buy, buying) a cap at the store.
Judy는 가게에서 모자를 사기 위해서 멈추어 섰다.

6 We tried (to climb, climbing) up the mountain.
우리는 그 산에 올라가려고 노력했다.

7 Tim stopped (to play, playing) PC games.
Tim은 컴퓨터 게임하는 것을 그만두었다.

8 I tried (to draw, drawing) the sunflowers.
나는 해바라기들을 시험 삼아 그려 보았다.

9 She remembers (to give, giving) him a ride tomorrow morning.
그녀는 내일 아침 그를 차 태워 줘야 할 것을 기억하고 있다.

10 Jason forgot (to call, calling) her back yesterday.
Jason은 어제 그녀에게 응답 전화해야 할 것을 잊어 버렸다.

drop by ~에 들르다   pull out the plug 코드를 빼다   sunflower 해바라기   give A a ride A를 차 태워주다

다음 주어진 단어를 이용하여 우리말에 알맞게 문장을 완성해 보자.

1 He sometimes forgets *to lock* the car door. (lock)

그는 가끔 자동차 문 잠그는 것을 잊는다.

2 Can I try _____ this bike? (ride)

시험 삼아 이 자전거를 타 보아도 될까요?

3 The child doesn't remember _____ in America. (live)

그 아이는 미국에서 살았던 것을 기억하지 못하고 있다.

4 He remembers _____ his hair cut today. (get)

그는 오늘 머리를 자를 것을 기억하고 있다.

5 Sally stopped _____ a taxi. (catch)

Sally는 택시를 잡기 위해서 멈추어 섰다.

6 Did you try _____ the math problem? (solve)

너는 그 수학 문제를 풀어 보려고 시도해 보았니?

7 James stopped _____ some money from ATM. (draw)

James는 현금자동인출기에서 약간의 돈을 인출하기 위해 멈췄다.

8 He remembers _____ his grandmother last weekend. (meet)

그는 지난 주말에 그의 할머니를 만난 것을 기억하고 있다.

9 Don't forget _____ your seatbelt. (fasten)

안전벨트 매는 것을 잊지 마라.

10 Dad doesn't forget _____ her birthday present. (buy)

아빠는 그녀의 생일 선물을 사오신다는 것을 잊지 않고 계신다.

ATM 현금자동 인출기   draw 인출하다   fasten 매다(채우다)   seatbelt 좌석벨트   present 선물

다음 주어진 단어를 이용하여 우리말에 알맞게 문장을 완성해 보자.

1 My grandfather *forgot* *wearing* his glasses. (wear)

나의 할아버지는 안경을 쓰고 계시다는 것을 잊었다.

2 You may _____ this button. (press)

너는 시험 삼아 이 단추를 눌러 보아도 좋다.

3 He doesn't _____ a promise. (break)

그는 약속을 어긴 것을 기억하지 못한다.

4 His uncle didn't _____ this morning. (shave)

그의 삼촌은 오늘 아침 면도해야 한다는 것을 잊지 않았다.

5 She _____ coffee suddenly. (drink)

그녀는 커피 마시는 것을 갑자기 그만두었다.

6 Did you _____ English? (master)

너는 영어를 정복하려고 노력해 보았니?

7 The kitten _____ down from the roof. (jump)

그 새끼 고양이는 지붕에서 아래로 시험 삼아 뛰어내려 보았다.

8 We _____ TV for dinner. (watch)

우리는 저녁을 먹기 위해 TV 보는 것을 그만두었다.

9 I _____ a house key with me. (take)

나는 집 열쇠를 가지고 가는 것을 잊었다.

10 Aron _____ to the hospital early tomorrow morning. (go)

Aron은 내일 아침 일찍 병원에 가야 한다는 것을 기억하고 있다.

press 누르다, 압력을 주다   shave 면도하다   suddenly 갑자기   master 정복하다   house key 집 열쇠

2 동명사의 의미상의 주어, 동명사의 부정

1 동명사의 의미상의 주어

동명사의 실제 행위자를 나타내는 말로서 이를 동명사의 의미상의 주어라고 한다.

● 문장의 주어와 동명사의 의미상의 주어가 같을 때

의미상의 주어를 생략한다.

ex. He enjoys ~~his~~ skiing. 그는 크커 스키 타는 것을 즐긴다.

● 문장의 주어와 동명사의 주어가 다를 때

동명사의 의미상의 주어를 반드시 써 주어야 하며, 그 위치는 동명사 바로 앞에 온다.

ex. I like   singing. 나는 노래하는 것을 좋아한다.
I like her singing. 나는 그녀가 노래하는 것을 좋아한다.

Tip! 동명사도 그 근본이 동사에 뿌리를 두고 있기 때문에 동사의 성질을 가지고 있다. 따라서 영어의 어순은 '주어 + 동사'의 형태이므로 동명사의 주어는 동명사 바로 앞에 온다고 생각하면 된다.

동명사의 의미상의 주어는 소유격이나 목적격을 써준다.

ex. I love his dancing. 나는 그가 춤추는 것을 좋아한다.
= I love him dancing.

● 동명사의 의미상의 주어의 생략

동명사의 주어가 일반인(we, you, they, people...)인 경우 생략한다.

ex. Seeing is believing. 보는 것이 믿는 것이다.

2 동명사의 부정

● 동명사 바로 앞에 not, never, no를 붙인다.

ex. Mom likes his not playing PC games any more.
엄마는 그가 더 이상 PC 게임을 하지 않는 것을 좋아하신다.

주어진 문장을 우리말로 옮겨 보자.

1 I like singing.

나는   *노래하는 것을*   좋아한다.

I like your singing.

나는   *네가 노래하는 것을*   좋아한다.

2 Bruce minds cooking.

Bruce는   꺼려한다.

Bruce minds Jane's cooking.

Bruce는   꺼려한다.

3 Tom loves wearing casual dress.

Tom은   무척 좋아한다.

Tom loves her wearing casual dress.

Tom은   무척 좋아한다.

4 My mother is proud of her son's speaking English well.

나의 어머니는   자랑스러워하신다.

My mother is proud of speaking English well.

나의 어머니는   자랑스러워하신다.

---

casual dress 평상복   **be proud of** ~을 자랑스러워하다

우리말을 영어로 옮겨 보자. (동명사 사용, 두개 가능)

1 She dislikes _his(him) telling_ a lie. (tell)

그녀는 그가 거짓말 하는 것을 싫어한다.

She dislikes _telling_ a lie.

그녀는 거짓말 하는 것을 싫어한다.

2 Mom minds meat a lot. (eat)

엄마는 내가 고기를 많이 먹는 것을 꺼려하신다.

Mom minds meat a lot.

엄마는 고기를 많이 먹는 것을 꺼려하신다.

3 Ann likes . (cook)

Ann은 요리하는 것을 좋아한다.

Ann likes .

Ann은 그 쉐프가 요리하는 것을 좋아한다.

4 He is interested in toy cars. (collect)

그는 장난감 자동차 모으기에 관심이 있다.

He is interested in toy cars.

그는 그의 딸이 장난감 자동차 모으는 것에 관심이 있다.

toy car 장난감 자동차

주어진 단어를 알맞은 형태로 바꾸어 문장을 완성해 보자. (동명사 사용, 두 개 가능)

1 I didn't feel *his (him)*   *stealing*   a glance at me. (he, steal)

2 Jim noticed   a surprise party. (we, throw)

3 He doesn't like   all day. (she, nag)

4 Liz isn't sure of   her out. (he, ask)

5 Does dad like   over night? (we, sit up)

6 Do you know   his own business? (he, start)

7 I was impressed by   the poor. (she, love)

8 Do you mind   you all the time? (the teacher, scold)

9 I remember   me on this issue. (Mary, advise)

10 Laura doesn't like   golf. (he, play)

steal a glance at ~을 훔쳐보다   notice 눈치채다, 알아차리다   nag 잔소리하다   sit up over night 밤새도록 안자고 있다
ask out 데이트 신청하다   the poor 가난한 사람들   impressed 감명을 받은

다음 주어진 단어를 알맞은 형태로 바꾸어 문장을 완성해 보자. (동명사 사용, 두 개 가능)

1 I am sure of _his(him) succeeding_ . (succeed)

나는 그가 성공할 것을 확신한다.

2 He remembers _____ so. (say)

그는 Jane이 그렇게 말한 것을 기억한다.

3 She loves _____ the guitar. (play)

그녀는 기타 치는 것을 무척 좋아한다.

4 Mothers like _____ for a long time. (sleep)

어머니들은 아기들이 오래 자는 것을 좋아한다.

5 He is interested in _____ . (study)

그는 그의 아들이 공부하는 것에 관심이 있다.

6 I was afraid of _____ married. (get)

나는 그가 결혼하는 것에 대해 염려했다.

7 Mary hates _____ clothes. (wash)

Mary는 빨래하는 것을 무척 싫어한다.

8 After _____ that, I went out. (say)

그녀가 그렇게 말한 후 나는 나왔다.

9 Paul didn't listen to _____ . (warn)

Paul은 그녀가 경고하는 것을 들으려 하지 않았다.

10 What do you think of _____ a designer? (become)

너는 디자이너가 되는 것에 대해서 어떻게 생각하니?

---

be sure of 확신하다   be fond of 좋아하다

다음 영어를 우리말로 옮겨 보자.

1 Not giving up is very important for us.

포기하지 않는 것은   우리에게 매우 중요하다.

2 He was ashamed of not knowing much.

그는   부끄러워했다.

3 Her hope is not being sick longer.

그녀의 희망은   이다.

4 Not knowing her is good for you.

너에게 좋은 것이다.

5 Not paying attention to the teacher is a bad habit.

나쁜 습관이다.

다음 주어진 단어를 이용하여 동명사의 부정문을 만들어 보자.

1 Would you mind opening the window? (not)

→ *Would you mind not opening the window?*   .

2 He regrets learning how to swim. (not)

→   .

3 There is telling what will happen tomorrow. (no)

→   .

4 Going out at night is safe. (never)

→   .

5 Skipping breakfast helps to lose weight. (not)

→   .

---

be ashamed of ~을 부끄러워하다   longer 더 이상   pay attention to ~에 주목하다, ~에 주의를 기울이다
regret 후회하다   there is no telling ~를 모른다   go out 외출하다

UNIT 3

전치사의 목적어로 쓰이는 동명사, 동명사를 이용한 주요 구문

1 전치사의 목적어로서의 동명사

🔹 전치사의 목적어로 동명사가 온다.

be interested in ~ing	~에 관심 있다
thank A for ~ing	A에게 ~에 대해 감사하다
be fond of ~ing	~을 좋아하다
be proud of ~ing	~을 자랑스러워하다
be good (bad/poor) at ~ing	~을 잘(못)한다
be afraid of ~ing	~을 두려워(염려)하다
be worried about ~ing	~에 대해 걱정(근심)하다
look forward to ~ing	~하는 것을 고대하다
be tired of ~ing	~하는 것이 지겹다 (싫증나다)

ex. He is interested in cooking noodle. 그는 국수 요리하는데 관심이 있다.
~~He is interested in to cook noodle.~~

2 동명사를 이용한 주요 구문

🔹 아래의 것들은 동명사를 이용하여 숙어로 사용된다.

be busy ~ing	~하느라 바쁘다
feel like ~ing	~하고 싶다
go ~ing	~하러 가다 (운동, 레저, 쇼핑)
cannot help ~ing	~하지 않을 수 없다
spend + 시간(돈) ~ing	~하는 데 시간(돈)을 보내다 (쓰다)
be worth ~ing	~할 가치가 있다

ex. She is busy washing the dishes. 그녀는 설거지하느라 바쁘다.
~~She is busy to wash the dishes.~~

Tip! go~ing는 주로 운동이나 레저, 쇼핑에 관련된 표현에 사용된다.

우리말에 알맞은 것을 보기에서 골라 보자.

| 보기 |

A. be proud of ~ing
B. go ~ing
C. be afraid of ~ing
D. feel like ~ing
E. thank A for ~ing
F. cannot help ~ing
G. look forward to ~ing
H. be worried about~ing
I. be interested in ~ing
J. be worth ~ing
K. spend + 시간(돈)~ing
L. be good (bad/poor) at ~ing
M. be busy ~ing
N. be fond of ~ing
O. be tired of ~ing

1 ~하러 가다   *B*

2 A에게 ~에 대해 감사하다

3 ~하는 것이 지겹다

4 ~하고 싶다

5 ~을 자랑스러워하다

6 ~하는 데 시간(돈)을 보내다(쓰다)

7 ~을 잘(못)한다

8 ~하지 않을 수 없다

9 ~에 관심 있다

10 ~하느라 바쁘다

11 ~을 좋아하다

12 ~을 두려워(염려)하다

13 ~을 갈망하다, 고대하다

14 ~할 가치가 있다

15 ~에 대해 걱정(근심)하다

주어진 단어를 이용하여 우리말에 알맞게 문장을 완성해 보자.

1 Tom _draws_ a rocket perfectly. (draw)

Tom은 로켓트를 완벽하게 그린다.

2 Jane is proud of _____ the gold medal. (win)

Jane은 금메달을 딴 것을 자랑스러워한다.

3 I feel like _____ a job. (get)

나는 일자리 얻고 싶다.

4 He cannot help _____ Bill. (invite)

그는 Bill을 초대하지 않을 수 없다.

5 She is busy _____ . (shop)

그녀는 쇼핑하느라 바쁘다.

6 The child wanted _____ a Teddy bear. (buy)

그 아이는 테디 베어를 사고 싶어 했다.

7 This bracelet is worth _____ . (keep)

이 팔찌는 보관할 가치가 있다.

8 He is worried about _____ a car. (drive)

그는 차 운전하는 것에 대해서 걱정한다.

9 Georgy let me _____ a Coke. (drink)

Georgy는 내가 콜라 한 잔 마시도록 내버려 두었다.

10 Dad goes _____ golf on Sundays. (play)

아빠는 일요일마다 골프 치러 가신다.

perfectly 완벽하게

주어진 단어를 이용하여 우리말에 알맞게 문장을 완성해 보자. (두 개 가능)

1 The child _is afraid of facing_ a dog. (face)

그 아이는 개와 마주치는 것을 두려워한다.

2 Tom with his family next week. (fish)

Tom은 다음 주 그의 가족들과 함께 낚시하러 갈 예정이다.

3 The boys PC games. (play)

그 소년들은 PC 게임 하느라고 바쁘다.

4 I something cold. (drink)

나는 찬 것을 좀 마시고 싶다.

5 He ramyen. (cook)

그는 라면 끓이는 것을 잘 못한다.

6 Jane at the picture. (laugh)

Jane은 그 사진을 보고 웃지 않을 수 없다.

7 Mom my brother again. (see)

엄마는 나의 오빠를 다시 만나볼 것을 고대하고 있다.

8 The book . (read)

그 책은 읽어볼 만한 가치가 있다.

9 We us. (help)

우리는 그녀가 우리를 도와 준 것에 대해서 감사했다.

10 She a diplomat. (be)

그녀는 외교관이 된 것을 자랑스러워한다.

---

face 마주치다   ramyen 라면   diplomat 외교관

다음 주어진 단어를 이용하여 우리말에 알맞게 문장을 완성해 보자.

1 She *was looking forward to meeting* her mom. (meet)

그녀는 그녀의 엄마를 만나기를 고대하고 있었다.

2 I _____ home now. (go)

나는 이제 집에 가고 싶다.

3 English _____ well. (learn)

영어는 잘 배울 가치가 있다.

4 I _____ on a field trip. (go)

나는 현장학습을 갈 것을 염려한다.

5 My uncle _____ yesterday. (hike)

나의 삼촌은 어제 하이킹하러 갔다.

6 Joe _____ for the mid-term test. (study)

Joe는 중간고사를 대비해서 공부하느라고 바쁘다.

7 My mom _____ soap opera every day. (watch)

나의 엄마는 날마다 연속극을 보는 데 2시간을 보내신다.

8 She _____ some salt in the soup. (put)

그녀는 수프에 약간의 소금을 넣지 않을 수 없다.

9 He _____ jump rope. (play)

그는 줄넘기를 잘 한다.

10 The woman _____ about others. (fond, talk)

그 여자는 다른 사람들에 대해 이야기 하는 것을 좋아한다.

---

go on a field trip 현장학습을 가다　　soap opera 연속극　　play jump rope 줄넘기하다

01 빈칸에 알맞은 것을 고르시오.

> *A* : Do you remember _____ her?
> *B* : No, I don't. Then I will call her soon.

① call
② to call
③ calling
④ called
⑤ to calling

02 다음 빈칸에 알맞은 것으로 짝지어진 것은?

> • He loves _____ dancing.
> • I can't stand _____ nagging.

① she - him
② her - she
③ her - he
④ hers - his
⑤ her - his

nag 잔소리하다

03 빈칸에 알맞은 것을 고르시오.

> Betty has no food. She regrets _____ food.

① not save
② not to save
③ not saving
④ saving
⑤ to save

regret 후회하다

04 다음 빈칸에 들어갈 동사의 형태로 알맞은 것은?

> They can not help _____ their homework.

① do
② did
③ doing
④ to do
⑤ does

[05–06] 빈칸에 알맞은 말을 |보기|에서 골라 쓰시오.

| 보기 |

for, like, of

05 Joseph feels _____ playing the guitar.

06 Daniel is proud _____ climbing up Mt. Everest.

Mt. Everest 에베레스트산

07 빈칸에 알맞은 말을 고르시오.

Sally : What are you doing?
Tony : I am spending 3 hours _____ a storybook.

① write
② to write
③ writing
④ wrote
⑤ written

08 (   ) 안의 동사를 알맞은 형태로 바꾸시오.

She is fond of (shop) with mom.

shop → _____

09 다음 문장 중 바른 것을 고르시오.

① The boys stopped to play football because of raining.
② How about take a walk?
③ I remember to see him last year.
④ Tommy remembered meeting her tomorrow.
⑤ He went out without saying goodbye.

10 빈칸에 들어갈 전치사로 알맞은 것을 고르시오.

• I am afraid _____ hurting you.

① out
② on
③ to
④ of
⑤ in

11 우리말과 일치하도록 빈칸에 알맞은 말을 쓰시오.

아빠는 내가 공부하는 것을 좋아한다.
→ Dad likes _____ studying.

12 어법에 맞지 <u>않는</u> 것을 고르시오.

> Susan is interested in ① <u>drawing</u> paintings. And she likes ② <u>to draw</u> with me. Because I am good at ③ <u>draw</u>. She is ④ <u>looking</u> forward to ⑤ <u>drawing</u> with me next weekend.

13 빈칸에 들어갈 말로 알맞은 것을 고르시오.

> Tony enjoys _____ baseball on weekends.

① play
② playing
③ to play
④ played
⑤ to played

14 다음 밑줄 친 부분이 바르게 쓰인 것을 고르시오.

① She is poor <u>at cooking</u>.
② The dog is good <u>to catching a ball</u>.
③ Jerry is interested <u>on collecting</u> stamps.
④ Peter is fond <u>in writing</u>.
⑤ Tom is afraid <u>to going</u> out.

15 다음 문장과 내용이 어울리는 것을 고르시오.

> Helen stopped to chat with her friends.

① Helen stopped chatting with her friends.
② Helen did not chat with her friends.
③ Helen stopped and began to chat with her friends.
④ Helen chatted with her friends without stopping.
⑤ Helen did not want to chat with her friends.

16 다음 두 문장의 의미가 서로 같지 <u>않은</u> 것은?

① His hobby is to collect dolls.
= His hobby is collecting dolls.
② Working is not easy.
= To work is not easy.
③ Ted began to play tennis.
= Ted began playing tennis.
④ Mary loves to swim.
= Mary loves swimming.
⑤ I forgot to close the window.
= I forgot closing the window.

다음 대화를 읽고 물음에 답하시오.

Maria : What do you want ⓐ to do today?

Rosa : I feel ⓑ in playing video game. Do you think that Linda will ⓒ let us play with her video games?

Maria : Why don't we give her a call? Because she is very nice, I think she will.

Rosa : Really? Can I use your cell phone, Jack? As mine is out of batteries, it is not working.

Jack : Of course, you can use my phone. Maybe she is ⓓ shopping now. Usually she spends a lot of time ⓔ buying something on Saturday.

---

17 밑줄 친 ⓐ~ⓔ에서 어법에 맞지 <u>않는</u> 것을 고르시오.

① ⓐ
② ⓑ
③ ⓒ
④ ⓓ
⑤ ⓔ

18 우리말과 일치하도록 할 때 not이 들어갈 위치로 알맞은 곳은?

Tom은 그 때 그녀에게 전화하지 못한 것을 기억하고 있다.

→ Tom ① remembers ② calling ③ her ④ then ⑤.

[19–20] 밑줄 친 곳에 알맞은 말을 고르시오.

19

Yesterday, I was busy _____ on the Internet.

---

① surf
② to surf
③ surfing
④ sured
⑤ to surfing

20

I thanked God _____ helping my dad.

---

① in
② of
③ on
④ to
⑤ for

01 다음 빈칸에 알맞은 것으로 짝지어진 것은?

> · He loves _____ smiling at him.
> · Mom dislikes _____ playing PC games.

① she - him
② she - he
③ her - he
④ hers - his
⑤ her - his

[03-04] 다음 중 맞는 표현에 O표하시오.

03

> He tried (to forget / forgetting) her. 그는 그녀를 잊으려고 노력했다. (아직 잊지 못했음.)

04

> She remembers (to visit / visiting) Mr. Park. 그녀는 Mr. Park을 만났던 것을 기억한다. (이미 Mr. Park을 만났음.)

02 다음 문장을 바르게 해석한 것을 고르시오.

> He stopped playing music.

① 그는 음악을 연주하기 위해 멈췄다.
② 그는 음악을 껐다.
③ 그는 음악을 연주하던 것을 멈췄다.
④ 그는 더 이상 음악을 연주할 수 없다.
⑤ 그는 음악을 연주해본 적이 없다.

05 다음 대화를 읽고 빈칸에 들어갈 알맞은 말을 고르시오.

> A : What is your interest?
> B : I am interested in _____.

① making movies
② make movies
③ to make movies
④ to making movies
⑤ to movies making

06 다음 괄호 안의 단어가 들어갈 알맞은 위치를 고르시오.

> (her)
> ① I ② love ③ to hear ④ singing
> ⑤ songs.
> 나는 그녀가 노래하는 것을 듣기를 무척 좋아한다.

07 다음 밑줄 친 단어와 바꿔 쓸 수 있는 단어를 고르시오.

> She loves <u>my</u> cooking.

① me
② mine
③ I
④ myself
⑤ her

08 다음 문장에서 생략 가능한 단어를 고르시오.

> People's knowing is power.
> 아는 것이 힘이다.

① people's
② knowing
③ is
④ power
⑤ 없음

09 다음 중 어색한 문장을 고르시오.

① Dad wants us to be healthy.
② She saw you working.
③ He promised she leaving.
④ Seeing is believing.
⑤ I love seeing Picasso's painting.

10 다음 중 밑줄 친 부분이 어색한 문장을 고르시오.

① We are tired of <u>waiting</u>.
② I am fond of <u>cooking</u>.
③ He is interested in <u>drawing</u>.
④ She is bad at <u>keeping</u> promises.
⑤ It is lucky to <u>being</u> on time.

11 다음 빈 칸에 공통으로 들어갈 단어를 고르시오.

> · My dad was proud ____ my
>   winning the award.
> · I am afraid ____ people's talking
>   about me.

① at
② about
③ in
④ for
⑤ of

12 다음 중 옳은 문장을 고르시오.

① She is busy to make dinner.
② I feel like to sleep.
③ He planned to study abroad.
④ I cannot help to cry.
⑤ She spent money to buy clothes.

13 다음 주어진 단어를 알맞게 변형하여 문장을 완성하시오.

> Anna thanked her parents so much
> for _____ her. (support)

support 지지하다

[14–15] 다음 글을 읽고 물음에 답하시오.

> This is my summer vacation. But I am
> busy ⓐ (do) a lot of things. Every
> morning, I go to a gym and exercise.
> After exercise, I go to a library and read
> books. ⓑ It is _____ my time
> studying and exercising.
> (공부하고 운동하는 데 나의 시간을 쓰는 것은 그럴 만한
> 가치가 있다.)

14 ⓐ의 괄호 안의 단어를 알맞은 형태로 바꿔 보시오.

ⓐ do → _____

15 ⓑ의 빈칸을 우리말에 맞게 채운 것을 고르시오.

① worth to spend
② worth spending
③ worth of spend
④ worth to spending
⑤ worth of spending

16 다음 문장에서 밑줄 친 부분을 바르게 고치시오.

> She loves <u>he</u> taking photos for her.

he → _____

17 다음 두 문장의 의미가 서로 같지 <u>않은</u> 것은?

① His hobby is to collect coins.
　= His hobby is collecting coins.
② Getting a job is not easy.
　= To get a job is not easy.
③ Jin began to play golf.
　= Jin began playing golf.
④ Ted loves to ski.
　= Ted loves skiing.
⑤ I forgot to send a mail.
　= I forgot sending a mail.

18 어법에 맞지 <u>않는</u> 것을 고르시오.

Ben is interested in ①<u>composing</u> music. He looked forward to ② <u>meet</u> my mom, because she is a famous composer. He ③<u>thanked</u> me for ④<u>giving</u> an opportunity. I was proud of both ⑤<u>Ben and my mom</u>.

compose 작곡하다

[19~20] 다음 대화를 읽고 물음에 답하시오.

Susan : I am told that you are going to Psy's concert.
Peter : Yes, the concert is next Sunday.
Susan : What do you like about Psy?
Peter : I like ⓐ _____ ⓑ _____ exciting music and dance.
Susan : The ticket must be very expensive.
Peter : Right, but it was ⓒ _____ the money. (그것은 그 돈을 쓸 만한 가치가 있었어.) I'm looking forward to seeing him perform.
Susan : Enjoy yourself.

19 ⓐ와 ⓑ에 각각 들어갈 말이 바르게 짝지어진 것을 고르시오.

① his - perform
② his - performed
③ he - performing
④ him - performing
⑤ him - perform

perform 공연하다

20 ⓒ에 들어갈 말로 가장 적절한 것을 고르시오.

① worth to spending
② worth to spend
③ worth spending
④ worth spend
⑤ worth by spending

Chapter 4

UNIT 1

분사구문의 종류

분사구문이란?
부사절에서 접속사와 주어를 없애고 분사를 이용하여 간단하게 부사구로 나타낸
형태를 말한다.

🔷 시간 : ~할 때 (when), ~하는 동안에 (while), ~한 후에 (after), ~하기 전에 (before)

ex. When I watched TV, I heard him come.

= (When) watching TV, I heard him come. TV를 보고 있었을 때, 나는 그가 오는 것을 들었다.

시간을 나타내는 분사구문은 보통 접속사를 생략하지 않는다.

🔷 이유 : ~하기 때문에, ~해서(~이므로) (because, since, as)

ex. Because he was busy, he couldn't finish the work.

= Being busy, he couldn't finish the work. 바빴기 때문에, 그는 그 일을 끝마칠 수 없었다.

Tip! 이유를 나타내는 접속사는 그 강약에 따라서 약간의 의미 차이가 있다. 실제로 영어에서는 as가 가장 많이 사용된다.
since는 자주 사용되지 않는다.

🔷 조건 : (만일) ~한다면 (if)

ex. If she meets him again, she will be very happy.

= Meeting him again, she will be very happy.
만일 그를 다시 만난다면, 그녀는 매우 행복할 것이다.

🔷 양보 : (비록) ~일지라도 (though)

ex. Though she meets him again, she will not be happy.

= Meeting him again, she will not be happy.
비록 그를 다시 만날지라도, 그녀는 행복하지 않을 것이다.

🔷 동시 동작 : ~하면서 (while)

ex. While he listens to music, he does his homework.

= Listening to music, he does his homework.
(그는) 음악을 들으면서, 그는 그의 숙제를 한다.

다음 중 알맞은 것을 골라 보자.

1 Having dinner, he takes a bath.

저녁을 (먹기 때문에, 먹는다면, 먹고 난 후에)

2 Seeing her daughter, she didn't get better.

그녀의 딸을 (보면서, 비록 보았을지라도, 본다면)

3 Hurrying up, we will not miss the airplane.

(서둘렀기 때문에, 서두른다면, 서둘렀을지라도)

4 Swimming in the pool, she got cold.

풀장에서 수영을 (할지라도, 한다면, 한 후에)

5 Being weak, Paul started to exercise.

(몸이 약하다면, 몸이 약하기 때문에, 몸이 약해진 동안에)

6 Feeling thirsty, Sarah bought a bottle of Coke from the store.

(목이 마른 후에, 목이 마를 지라도, 목이 말라서)

7 Getting fat, she started a diet.

(살이 찌므로, 살이 찐다면, 살이 찌더라도)

8 Opening the piano, he practiced for an hour.

피아노를 (연다면, 연 후에, 열면서)

9 Driving his car, dad listens to the news.

그의 차를 (운전하기 때문에, 운전할지라도, 운전하면서)

10 Turning on the TV, she sat on the couch.

TV를 (켠 후에, 켠다면, 켤지라도)

miss 놓치다   diet 다이어트(식이요법)   practice 연습하다

다음 중 밑줄 친 곳의 알맞은 우리말을 골라 보자.

1 Being in middle school, he lived in London.

중학교에 (다녔기 때문에, 다녔을 때, 다녔다면)

2 Sleeping on the sofa, Anne had a nice dream.

소파에서 (잔다면, 자고 있는 동안에, 잔 후에)

3 Seeing her again, I will be glad.

그녀를 다시 (만난다면, 만나서, 만날지라도)

4 Seeing her again, I will not be glad at all.

그녀를 다시 (만난다면, 만나서, 만날지라도)

5 Brushing her hair every morning, she goes to school.

매일 아침 머리를 (빗으면서, 빗을지라도, 빗은 후에)

6 Living in the countryside, she has few friends in Seoul.

시골에 (산다면, 살지라도, 살고 있으므로)

7 Whistling merrily, Tommy is washing his car.

즐겁게 (휘파람을 불면서, 휘파람을 분 후에, 휘파람을 불기 때문에)

8 Being 10 years old, she can read the English newspaper.

10살 (인 동안에, 일지라도, 이라면)

9 Being honest, David got loved by all.

정직 (하다면, 할지라도, 하기 때문에)

10 Staying here, you may read my books.

여기에 (머무는 동안에, 머문 후에, 머물지라도)

at all 전혀   **whistle** 휘파람을 불다

기본 TEST

다음 밑줄 친 곳을 우리말로 옮기고, 분사 구문의 쓰임을 골라 보자.

1 <u>Breaking</u> the vase, Jason got scolded.   (시간, (원인), 조건, 양보, 동시동작)

꽃병을   *깨기 때문에*   .

2 <u>Hearing</u> her news, Fred will call her instantly.   (시간, 원인, 조건, 양보, 동시동작)

그녀의 소식을   .

3 <u>Flying</u> away from the branch, the magpie chirped.   (시간, 원인, 조건, 양보, 동시동작)

나뭇가지로 부터   .

4 <u>Having</u> an expensive bike, she can't ride it well.   (시간, 원인, 조건, 양보, 동시동작)

비록 비싼 자전거를   .

5 <u>Lending</u> some money to Jane, she regreted it soon.   (시간, 원인, 조건, 양보, 동시동작)

Jane에게 돈을 좀   .

6 <u>Getting</u> my sister's help, I can solve the problems.   (시간, 원인, 조건, 양보, 동시동작)

만일 나의 누나의 도움을   .

7 <u>Losing</u> the car key, Ann could not drive her car.   (시간, 원인, 조건, 양보, 동시동작)

자동차 열쇠를   .

8 <u>Waving</u> its tail, the dog came running to us.   (시간, 원인, 조건, 양보, 동시동작)

꼬리를   .

9 <u>Crossing</u> the street, my grandmother is very careful.   (시간, 원인, 조건, 양보, 동시동작)

길을   .

10 <u>Making a noise</u> in class, they were punished.   (시간, 원인, 조건, 양보, 동시동작)

수업 시간에   .

---

scold 야단치다   **instantly** 즉시   **magpie** 까치   **chirp** 지저귀다   **for a long time** 오랫동안
regret 후회하다   **wave** 흔들다   **tail** 꼬리   **punish** 벌주다   **make a noise** 시끄럽게 떠들다

UNIT 2

분사 구문 만들기

접속사가 있는 문장을 부사절이라고 하고 접속사가 없는 문장을 주절이라고 한다.

🟦 **부사절과 주절의 주어가 같고 둘의 동사의 시제가 같은 경우**

- 부사절의 주어와 접속사를 없앤다.
- 부사절의 동사의 원형에 **ing**를 붙인다.
- 주절은 그대로 써 준다.

ⓐ 부사절 – 현재, 주절 – 현재

ex. When she eats dinner , she talks with him.
      현재   현재

= – – Eating dinner , she talks with him.

저녁 식사를 할 때, 그녀는 그와 이야기를 한다.

Tip! 우리말에서도 주어를 반복해서 말하지 않는 것과 같이 주어를 없애고 말한다고 생각하면 이해하기가 쉽다.

ⓑ 부사절 – 과거, 주절 – 과거

ex. When she ate dinner , she talked with him.
      과거   과거

= – – Eating dinner , she talked with him.

저녁 식사를 할 때, 그녀는 그와 이야기를 했다.

ⓒ 부사절 – 현재 (속뜻 : 미래), 주절 – 미래

부사절이 현재이고 주절이 미래일 경우, 그 속뜻을 들여다보면 부사절이 현재일지라도 미래의 일을 이야기하므로 부사절과 주절의 시제는 같은 것이 된다.

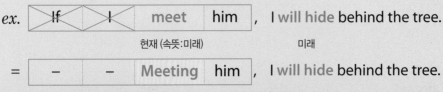

ex. If I meet him , I will hide behind the tree.
      현재 (속뜻:미래)   미래

= – – Meeting him , I will hide behind the tree.

그를 만난다면, 나는 나무 뒤에 숨을 것이다.

부사절의 접속사와 주어를 ×표 하고 빈칸을 채워 분사구문으로 만들어 보자.

1

~~When~~	~~I~~	solve	the math quiz

, I feel a headache.

→

–	–	*Solving*	*the math quiz*

, I feel a headache.

2

While	we	do	our homework

, we talk too much.

→

, we talk too much.

3

Because	he	exercises	everyday

, he is healthy.

→

, he is healthy.

4

While	she	took	a shower

, she sang loud.

→

, she sang loud.

5

When	they	ride	a bus

, they enjoy the scenery.

→

, they enjoy the scenery.

6

When	he	goes	out of his office

, he turns off the light.

→

, he turns off the light.

7

As	it	grew up

, it bore many fruits.

→

, it bore many fruits.

---

headache 두통　　scenery 경치　　bear (아이를) 낳다, (열매를) 맺다

부사절의 접속사와 주어를 ×표 하고, 분사구문으로 바꿔 보자.

1 ~~When I~~ watch a movie, I eat a lot of popcorn.

→ _Watching_ a movie, I eat a lot of popcorn.

2 Because he loved Kate, he couldn't say a word.

→ _____ Kate, he couldn't say a word.

3 As she lost her bag, she had no money.

→ _____ her bag, she had no money.

4 After I finish my homework, I will play the game.

→ _____ my homework, I will play the game.

5 Though I was in my room, I didn't open the door.

→ _____ in my room, I didn't open the door.

6 As he was sleepy, he went to bed early.

→ _____ sleepy, he went to bed early.

7 After she turned off her computer, she was reminded of his mail.

→ _____ her computer, she was reminded of his mail.

8 Because he was thirsty, he opened the refrigerator.

→ _____ thirsty, he opened the refrigerator.

9 When I go jogging, I will take my dog.

→ _____ jogging, I will take my dog.

10 Though she was a famous singer, she was not happy.

→ _____ a famous singer, she was not happy.

---

say a word 말 한마디 하다   **be remind of** ~이 생각나다   **thirsty** 목이 마른   **refrigerator** 냉장고

부사절의 접속사와 주어를 ×표 하고, 분사구문으로 바꿔 보자.

1 If you read many good books, you will be wiser.

→ _Reading many good books_ , you will be wiser.

2 When I take photos, I close my left eye.

→ , I close my left eye.

3 Though she is a miser, she spends a lot of money for her children.

→ , she spends a lot of money for her children.

4 When I fixed my computer, I was so relieved.

→ , I was so relieved.

5 After they play soccer under the sun, they rest in the shade.

→ , they rest in the shade.

6 If you go straight, you will find the bank.

→ , you will find the bank.

7 As he slipped on the ice, he was in pain.

→ , he was in pain.

8 While she took a walk, she thought of home.

→ , she thought of home.

9 As he sold all the fruits, he went back home.

→ , he went back home.

10 Because he was late for school, he was scolded by the teacher.

→ , he was scolded by the teacher.

---

miser 구두쇠 **relieved** 마음이 놓인 **shade** 그늘 **slip** 미끄러지다

UNIT 3 분사구문을 만들 때 유의사항, 분사 구문의 부정

1 부사절의 주어와 주절의 주어

🔷 주어는 서로 같지만, 부사절의 주어가 대명사가 아닌 경우

주절의 주어(대명사)를 부사절의 주어(고유명사/일반명사)로 바꾸어 주어야 한다.

ex. As Jane is lazy, she doesn't get a good grade.
> Jane은 게으르기 때문에, 그녀는 좋은 점수를 받지 못한다.

= Being lazy, Jane doesn't get a good grade.
> 게으르기 때문에, Jane은 좋은 점수를 받지 못한다.

이 때 Jane으로 바꾸어 써 주지 않으면 she가 누구인지 알 수 없다.

🔷 주어가 다를 경우

부사절의 주어를 그대로 남겨둔다.

ex. As it is too cold, we can't go out.
= It being too cold, we can't go out. 너무 춥기 때문에, 우리는 나갈 수 없다.

2 분사구문에서 being의 생략

🔷 부사절의 동사가 'be 동사'인 경우 : 분사구문에서 being은 생략 가능하다.

ex. As it is made in Korea, it is easy to use.
= Being made in Korea, it is easy to use. 한국에서 만들어졌으므로, 그것은 사용하기가 쉽다.
= Made in Korea, it is easy to use.

ex. As she was so sleepy, she went to bed early.
= Being so sleepy, she went to bed early. 그녀는 매우 졸리워서, 그녀는 일찍 자러 갔다.
= So sleepy, she went to bed early.

● 부사절의 동사가 진행형인 경우 : being은 반드시 생략한다.

ex. While he **is chewing** a gum, he plays baseball.
= **Chewing** a gum, he plays baseball. 그는 껌을 씹으면서 야구를 한다.
= ~~Being chewing a gum, he plays baseball.~~ (X)

Tip! 진행형에서 being을 그대로 살리면 'being chewing ~' 처럼 ~ing이 연속해서 반복되므로 어감이 매우 부자연스럽다.

3 접속사의 생략

● before

접속사 **before**는 생략하지 않는다.

ex. Before she goes out, she looks in the mirror.
= **Before** going out, she looks in the mirror. 그녀는 외출하기 전에 거울을 본다.
= ~~Going out, she looks in the mirror.~~ (X)

● when, while, after와 though

시간(when, while, after)과 양보(though)를 나타내는 접속사는, 문장의 뜻을 분명히 하기 위해서 많은 경우 남겨둔다.

ex. When he reads a book, he wears a glasses.
= Reading a book, he wears a glasses.
= **When** reading a book, he wears a glasses. (그는) 책을 읽을 때, 그는 안경을 쓴다.

ex. Though they lives in America, they can't speak English well.
= Living in America, they can't speak English well.
= **Though** living in America, they can't speak English well.
비록 (그들은) 미국에 살고 있을 지라도, 그들은 영어를 잘 못한다.

4 분사 구문의 부정

● not 또는 never를 분사(~ing, ~ed)의 앞에 놓는다.

ex. As he **didn't study** hard, he got the poor grade.
= **Not studying** hard, he got the poor grade. 열심히 공부하지 않았으므로, 그는 나쁜 점수를 받았다.

주절과 종속절의 주어에 ○표 하고, 분사구문으로 바꿔 보자.

1 When (Mr. Brown) snuck up to his sister, (he) surprised her.

= _Sneaking up_ to his sister, _Mr. Brown_ surprised her.

2 If Tom runs as usual, he will win the race.

= _____ as usual, _____ will win the race.

3 Though my friend is short, she is clever.

= _____ short, _____ is clever.

4 If dad eats cereal everyday, he will get tired of it.

= _____ cereal everyday, _____ will get tired of it.

5 When Mary heard her alarm, she woke up.

= _____ her alarm, _____ woke up.

6 As it was rainy, they canceled the concert.

= _____ rainy, they canceled the concert.

7 When it is foggy, we cannot drive on the highway.

= _____ foggy, we cannot drive on the highway.

---

sneak up 살금살금 다가가다   **as usual** 평소대로   **cereal** 씨리얼   **get tired of** ~에 권태를 느끼다/ 질리다

주절과 종속절의 주어에 ○표 하고, 분사구문으로 바꿔 보자.

1 Because (Jane) turned off her alarm, (she) overslept.

= *Turning off* her alarm, *Jane* overslept.

2 As he studied for 5 hours, he was very hungry.

= for 5 hours, was very hungry.

3 As it was too hot, we canceled our schedule.

= too hot, canceled our schedule.

4 When the mice saw the eagle, they ran into the hole.

= the eagle, ran into the hole.

5 Though plastic is light, it is strong.

= light, is strong.

6 While he washed the dishes, he listened to music.

= the dishes, listened to music.

7 If My sister finds her dog, she will be happy.

= her dog, will be happy.

8 Because she was too shy, she didn't talk to anyone.

= too shy, didn't talk to anyone.

9 While Bill has dinner, he watches the news.

= dinner, watches the news.

10 As she got presents on her birthday, she was happy.

= presents on her birthday, was happy.

---

oversleep 늦잠자다　cancel 취소하다　schedule 스케줄

주어진 문장을 분사구문으로 만들어 보자.

1 As he was too busy , he could not go out with his friends.

Being too busy , he could not go out with his friends.

Too busy , he could not go out with his friends.

2 When she shops with mom , she feels good.

, she feels good.

, she feels good.

3 As she was so frightened , she hid in her room.

, she hid in her room.

, she hid in her room.

4 While she was wrapping the CD , she thought of the boy friend.

, she thought of the boy friend.

, she thought of the boy friend.

5 If I find my ring again , I won't take it off.

, I won't take it off.

---

frighten 놀라게하다   hide 숨다

주어진 문장을 분사구문으로 만들 때, 부사절의 시제를 고르고 알맞은 것을 모두 골라 보자.

1 As It is hot now, he will take off his coat.   (현재), 진행, 과거)

→ It (be hot, hotting, (being hot)) now, he will take off his coat.

2 As he was running to catch the train, he didn't see the sign.   (현재, 진행, 과거)

→ (Being running, Running, Ran) to catch the train, he didn't see the sign.

3 While she was walking along the street, she smiled silently.   (현재, 진행, 과거)

→ (Being walking, Walking, Walked) along the street, she smiled silently.

4 As it is covered with snow, it is hard to climb.   (현재, 진행, 과거)

→ (Being covered, Being covering, Covered) with snow, it is hard to climb.

5 While Eli was combing her hair, she asked mom for breakfast.   (현재, 진행, 과거)

→ (Being combing, combed, Combing) her hair, Eli asked mom for breakfast.

6 As the mattress is filled with water, it is too cold.   (현재, 진행, 과거)

→ (Filled, Being filled, Filling) with water, the mattress is too cold.

7 When Maria was eating something, she heard the bell ring.   (현재, 진행, 과거)

→ (Being eating, Eating, Being eat) something, Maria heard the bell ring.

8 While he was taking a shower, he felt pleasant.   (현재, 진행, 과거)

→ (Being taking, Taking) a shower, he felt pleasant.

9 As she was sick very much, she had to stay in bed.   (현재, 진행, 과거)

→ (Being sick, Was sick, Sick) very much, she had to stay in bed.

10 As she was so tall, she had to bend down.   (현재, 진행, 과거)

→ (Being so tall, Be so tall, So tall), she had to bend down.

---

silently 조용히   mattress 매트리스   bend down (허리를) 굽히다

생략할 수 없는 접속사에 O표 해 보자.

1 (Before) going outside, she turns off the lights.

2 After having meals, he cleans the table.

3 Before moving to this city, Jimmy lived in LA.

4 When being too busy, I don't pick up the phone.

5 Though being cold outside, Anne was not wearing a sweater.

6 Before going to bed, I brush my teeth.

7 Before Julia buys a T-shirt, she always tries it on.

8 Before driving a car, you need to check the tires.

주어진 말을 이용하여 다음을 부정 분사 구문으로 만들 때, 빈칸에 알맞은 말을 써 보자.

1 As he didn't make a mistake, he got some pocket money. (not)

→ _____Not making_____ a mistake, he got some pocket money.

2 As we don't have any food in the refrigerator, we will eat out. (not)

→ _____ any food in the refrigerator, we will eat out.

3 Because dad didn't watch the news, he knew nothing about the outside world. (never)

→ _____ the news, dad knew nothing about the outside world.

4 If she doesn't practice the flute enough, she will ruin the contest. (not)

→ _____ the flute enough, she will ruin the contest.

5 Because he didn't wear the muffler, he got a sore throat. (not)

→ _____ the muffler, he got a sore throat.

---

ruin 망치다   sore 따끔따끔한   throat 목구멍   sore throat 인후염

다음 주어진 문장을 분사 구문으로 만들어 보자.

1 Before he gets exercise, he drinks some water.

   =   *Before getting*   exercise, he drinks some water.

2 Because it was covered with ants, it was hard to open.

   =   with ants, it was hard to open.

3 Before I forgot the phone number, I saved it on my cell-phone.

   =   the phone number, I saved it on my cell-phone.

4 As I looked at the calendar, I waited for the Christmas.

   =   the calendar, I waited for the Christmas.

5 Before she goes out, she looks in a mirror.

   =   out, she looks in a mirror.

6 Before David makes an appointment, he thinks twice.

   =   an appointment, David thinks twice.

7 Before you leave home, you should check the gas.

   =   home, you should check the gas.

8 If they forget to feed the dog, they will feel sorry.

   =   to feed the dog, they will feel sorry.

9 Before we believe him, we need to check his words.

   =   him, we need to check his words.

10 As he was playing video games, he didn't answer me.

   =   video games, he didn't answer me.

---

cover 덮다   ant 개미   calendar 달력   mirror 거울   gas (gasoline) 휘발유   believe 믿다

다음 주어진 문장을 분사구문으로 만들어 보자.

1 While we do our homework, we eat some snack.

= *While doing* our homework, we eat some snack.

= *Doing* our homework, we eat some snack.

2 After we walked on the muddy road, we got our sneakers dirty.

= on the muddy road, we got our sneakers dirty.

= on the muddy road, we got our sneakers dirty.

3 While she takes her final exam, she is nervous.

= her final exam, she is nervous.

= her final exam, she is nervous.

4 As she was bored yesterday, she borrowed a movie CD.

= yesterday, she borrowed a movie CD.

= yesterday, she borrowed a movie CD.

5 As Bill ate too much at the buffet, he had a stomachache.

= too much at the buffet, Bill had a stomachache.

6 If we exercise hard, we will get our clothes wet.

= hard, we will get our clothes wet.

---

muddy 진흙의   **nervous** 예민한   **buffet** 부페   **stomachache** 위통

[01–03] 빈칸에 들어갈 말로 가장 알맞은 것을 고르시오.

01

> When I take a bath, I listen to music.
> = _____ a bath, I listen to music.

① Being took
② Being taken
③ Being take
④ Taking
⑤ Be taking

02

> As Tom isn't sick, he can go camping.
> = _____ , Tom can go camping.

① Being sick not
② Not being sick
③ Being not sick
④ Not sicked
⑤ No being sick

03

> Before Mary goes to school, she checks school supplies.
> = _____to school, Mary checks school supplies.

① Going
② Being go
③ Before going
④ Be going
⑤ Mary going

04 분사구문으로 바꾸어 쓸 때 빈칸에 들어갈 알맞은 말을 쓰시오.

> 엄마의 충고를 따르지 않았기 때문에 나는 감기에 걸렸다.
> Because I didn't follow mom's advice, I caught a cold.
> → _____
> mom's advice, I caught a cold.

05 다음 빈칸에 알맞은 말을 고르시오.

> While Mike was preparing the concert, he didn't eat anything.
> = While preparing the concert, _____ didn't eat anything.

① he
② she
③ Mike
④ I
⑤ you

06 다음 빈칸에 알맞은 말을 고르시오.

> _____ the window, Christie found a pretty bird.

① Open
② Opened
③ Opening
④ Being open
⑤ Be open

07 밑줄 친 분사 구문이 바르게 쓰이지 <u>않은</u> 문장을 고르시오.

① <u>Because</u> being tired, he didn't say anything.
② <u>Before</u> going to the bathroom, I always wash my hands.
③ <u>After</u> finishing her homework, Christine went out.
④ <u>Though</u> knowing the truth, Judy will not tell them it.
⑤ <u>When</u> going out, Sandra doesn't forget to bring her handbag.

bathroom 화장실

[08–09] 밑줄 친 곳을 바르게 고쳐 쓰시오.

08

<u>Be</u> produced in China, the things are cheap.
중국에서 생산되었기 때문에, 그 물건들은 싸다.

_____Be_____ → _____

09

As Jimmy planned a trip to Italy, he was excited.
= Planning a trip to Italy, <u>he</u> was excited.

_____he_____ → _____

10 다음 중 부사절을 분사 구문으로 바르게 바꾸지 않은 것을 모두 고르시오.

① As Tom had some money, he bought fruits.
→ Having some money, Tom bought fruits.
② When I am wearing a white skirt, I feel like eating an ice cream.
→ Being wearing a white skirt, I feel like eating an ice cream.
③ Before I eat breakfast, I don't drink water.
→ Eating breakfast, I don't drink water.
④ After I finish homework, I will go swimming.
→ Finishing homework, I will go swimming.
⑤ As I didn't study hard, I couldn't pass the test.
→ Not studying hard, I couldn't pass the test.

11 아래 문장에서 'never'를 넣어야 할 자리를 고르시오.

As I was never the fastest, I couldn't become a good runner.
= ① Being ② the fastest, ③ I couldn't ④ become ⑤ a good runner.

12 우리말과 같은 뜻이 되도록 빈칸에 알맞은 말을 고르시오.

> 돈이 없어서, 우리는 집으로 걸어와야만 했다.
> = As we had no money, we had to walk home.
> = _____ no money, we had to walk home.

① Having
② Being had
③ As having
④ Having had
⑤ As had

13 빈칸에 알맞은 말로 바르게 짝지어진 것을 고르시오.

> · _____ able to see anything, Andy turned the light on.
> · When _____ the door, Cindy saw a weird sight.

① Being not - opened
② Being not - opening
③ Not being - opening
④ Not being - opened
⑤ Never being - opened

weird 기이한, 기괴한   sight 광경

14 빈칸에 알맞은 말을 고르시오.

> After _____ a new hat, Erin found her old one.

① buy
② buys
③ bought
④ to buy
⑤ buying

15 부사절을 분사 구문으로 바꾸어 써 보시오.

> As I didn't prepare for the meeting well, I missed a good chance.
> = _____ for the meeting well, I missed a good chance.

16 다음 문장에서 생략해야만 하는 것을 고르시오.

> ① Being ② watching ③ the movie, I ④ remembered my childhood.
> ⑤ 없음

[17–18] 다음 대화를 읽고 물음에 답하시오.

> *Andrew* : Do you know Paul well?
> *Ben* : Yes, he is my neighbor and best friend.
> *Andrew* : What does Paul do after school?
> *Ben* : ⓐ <u>Being an athlete</u>, he loves to watch sports on TV.
> *Andrew* : Paul sounds like a very interesting person. I would like to meet him.
> *Ben* : ⓑ <u>Finishing my homework</u>, I will meet Paul today. Do you want to come?
> *Andrew* : I'd love to!

17 밑줄 친 ⓐ를 접속사 As를 사용하여 부사절로 만들어 보시오.

→ As _____

athlete 운동선수

18 다음 문장은 밑줄 친 ⓑ를 부사절로 바꾼 것이다. 빈칸에 들어갈 접속사로 알맞은 것을 고르시오.

> _____ I finish my homework.

① Though
② After
③ While
④ And
⑤ Since

[19–20] 다음 글을 읽고 물음에 답하시오.

> Laura is a college student majoring in English. She is ready for a vacation. She is tired of studying and wants to go to a warm, sunny place. ⓐ great things about the Bahamas, she bought plane tickets yesterday.
> She is very excited about taking a break from school. ⓑ <u>While she waits for the vacation</u>, she dreams about how nice it will be.

19 밑줄 친 ⓐ에 들어갈 알맞은 말을 고르시오.

① Heard
② Being heard
③ Being hear
④ Hearing
⑤ Her heard

major in ~을 전공하다

20 밑줄 친 ⓑ를 분사 구문으로 만들 때, 빈칸에 알맞은 말을 쓰시오.

→ _____ , she dreams about how nice it will be.

[01–03] 다음 두 문장의 뜻이 같도록 빈칸에 알맞은 말을 고르시오.

01

> When I turned on the TV, I heard dad come.
> = _____ the TV, I heard dad come.

① Being turning on
② Turn on
③ Turning on
④ It I turn on
⑤ Turned on

02

> As she was angry, she didn't apologize.
> = _____ angry, she didn't apologize.

① Being
② Because
③ Be
④ She be
⑤ She was being

apologize 사과하다

03

> If we see you again, we will be very excited.
> = _____ you again, we will be very excited.

① See
② Seeing
③ While we see
④ Though we see
⑤ Being seeing

04 다음 문장에서 밑줄 친 부분을 바르게 고치시오.

> <u>Travel</u> Europe again, I will be very happy.
> 만일 내가 유럽을 다시 여행한다면, 나는 매우 행복할 것이다.

Travel → _____

[05–06] 다음 빈 칸에 알맞은 말을 써 넣으시오..

05

> As Kate was too tired, she stayed at home.
> = Being too tired, _____ stayed at home.

06

> As it was foggy, he couldn't drive a truck.
> = _____ being foggy, he couldn't drive a truck.

[07–09] 밑줄 친 곳을 바르게 고쳐 쓰시오.

07

Though they break up now, they will meet again.
= _____ up now, they will meet again.

비록 그들이 지금 헤어질지라도, 그들은 다시 만날 것이다.

① Breaking
② They breaking
③ Though breaking
④ Though break
⑤ Being break

08

As it is written in English, it is hard for me to read.
= _____ in English, it is hard for me to read.

① As be written
② It being written
③ Being written
④ Be written
⑤ Written

09

Before you go out, you should close the window.
= _____ out, you should close the window.

① Before going
② Going
③ Before go
④ To go
⑤ Being gone

10 다음에서 어색한 문장을 고르시오.

① When reading a book, mom wears a glasses.
② After having dinner, he takes a walk.
③ Before going to bed, I brushes my teeth.
④ While watching a movie, they eat popcorn.
⑤ Because walking too much, we are tired.

11 다음에서 알맞은 부정 분사구문을 고르시오.

> As she was not honest, she was unhappy in the end.
> = _____ , she was unhappy in the end.

① Being not honest
② Not being honest
③ Not be honest
④ Be not honest
⑤ Don't be honest

12 다음 빈칸에 들어갈 올바른 것을 고르시오.

> As it is too hot, we'll stay in the pool.
> = _____ being too hot, we'll stay in the pool.

① We
② That
③ They
④ It
⑤ 생략 가능

13 다음 중 밑줄 친 부분이 어색한 것을 고르시오.

① <u>Being made</u> in Korea, it was good.
② <u>Being tired</u>, she went to bed early.
③ <u>Being drinking</u> coffee, he works.
④ <u>Being too sad</u>, she started to cry.
⑤ <u>It being too cold</u>, water froze.

[14-15] 다음 글의 내용과 일치하지 <u>않는</u> 것을 고르시오..

> I have a friend, Laura, who came from Indonesia. She has been studying Korean since she was a high school student. Because learning Korean was not easy, she wanted to give up. But now she speaks Korean very well. I was so impressed. ⓐ <u>As I didn't know any foreign language</u>, I decided to learn one.

14 다음 글의 내용과 일치하지 <u>않는</u> 것을 고르시오.

① 내 친구 Laura는 인도네시아에서 왔다.
② 그녀는 고등학교 때부터 한국어를 공부했다.
③ 그녀는 한국어를 공부하는 것이 어렵지 않았다.
④ 그녀는 지금 한국말을 굉장히 잘한다.
⑤ 나도 외국어를 배울 것이다.

15 밑줄 친 ⓐ를 분사구문으로 바꾸어 쓰시오.

> As I didn't know any foreign language,
> → _____ any foreign language,

16 다음 빈칸에 들어갈 알맞은 말을 고르시오.

> After _____ a new ruler, she found her old one from her bag.

① buy
② bought
③ buying
④ to buy
⑤ buys

17 다음 밑줄 친 분사구문의 원래의 부사절 형태를 고르시오.

> <u>Being too late</u>, I had to take a taxi.

① As I am too late
② As I was too late
③ As I took late
④ As I got up late
⑤ As I had too late

18 괄호 안의 단어가 들어갈 알맞은 자리를 고르시오.

> (Not)
> ① Practicing ② hard, he ③ failed ④ his driver license exam ⑤.
> 열심히 연습하지 않았으므로, 그는 운전면허 시험에서 떨어졌다.

19 다음 밑줄 친 단어 중 생략할 수 없는 접속사를 고르시오.

① <u>Before</u> going out, she checked her hair again.
② <u>When</u> swimming, he wears glasses.
③ <u>Though</u> living in Paris, they don't go to museum.
④ <u>While</u> reading a book, she listens to music.
⑤ <u>After</u> watching a movie, we ate lunch.

20 빈칸에 공통으로 들어갈 말을 고르시오.

> · _____ being able to eat anything, I was so hungry.
> · _____ listening to dad's advice, I got a cold.

① While
② After
③ None
④ Not
⑤ When

Chapter 5

조동사

조동사란?

본동사를 도와 그 의미를 부분적으로 바꾸어 주는 (보)조동사를 말한다.

1 can

> 🧊 능력 / 허락 : ~할 수 있다 / ~해도 좋다

ⓐ 긍정문

〈능력〉 *ex.* He **can** swim for an hour. 그는 1시간 동안 수영을 할 수 있다.

이 때 **can**은 'be able to'로 바꾸어 쓸 수 있다.

ex. You can pass the exam. 너는 그 시험에 합격 할 수 있어.

= You **are able to** pass the exam.

〈허락〉 *ex.* You **can** go now. 너는 지금 가도 좋아.

이 때 can은 may로 바꾸어 쓸 수 있다.

ex. You **can** go home. 너는 집에 가도 좋아.

= You **may** go home.

ⓑ 부정문

〈불가능〉 *ex.* He **cannot** pass the exam. 그는 그 시험에 합격 할 수 없어.

= He **is not able to** pass the exam.

〈불허가〉 *ex.* You **cannot** use my pen. 너는 내 펜을 사용하면 안 돼.

= You **may not** use my pen.

ⓒ 의문문

〈능력〉 Can 주어 ~? : ~할 수 있니?

ex. **Can** he swim? 그는 수영을 할 수 있니? (수영 할 줄 아니?)

– Yes, he can.　　　– No, he can't.

ex. **Is** he able to swim?

– Yes, he is.　　　– No, he isn't.

〈허락〉 Can I ~? : ~해도 좋니?

ex. **Can I** use your computer? 네 컴퓨터를 좀 사용해도 되니?

이때 Can은 Could/May로 바꾸어 쓸 수 있다.

〈요청, 부탁〉 Can you ~? : ~해 주겠니?

       ex. Can you open the window? 창문 좀 열어 줄래?

           = Could you open the window? 창문 좀 열어 주시겠어요?

           = Will you open the window? 창문 좀 열어 줄래?

           = Would you open the window? 창문 좀 열어 주시겠어요?

〈긍정〉	〈부정〉
– OK. / Sure. / Certainly	– I'm sorry, but I can't ~.
– Yes, of course.	– I'd like to, but I can't ~.

Tip! Could you~/ Would you ~는 Can you~/ Will you~ 보다 정중한 표현이다.

2 may

추측 / 허락 : ~일지도 모른다 / ~해도 좋다

ⓐ 긍정문

〈추측〉 *ex.* It **may** rain tomorrow. 내일 비가 올지도 모른다.

〈허락〉 *ex.* You **may** go home. 너는 집에 가도 좋아.

          = You **can** go home.

ⓑ 부정문

〈부정적 추측〉 *ex.* It **may not** rain tomorrow. 내일 비가 오지 않을지도 모른다.

〈불허가〉 *ex.* You **may not** go out. 너는 밖에 나가면 안된다.

          = You **can not** go out.

ⓒ 의문문

〈허락〉 *ex.* **May I** use your computer? 당신의 컴퓨터를 좀 사용해도 좋을까요?

          = **Can I** use your computer? 네 컴퓨터를 좀 사용해도 되니?

          = **Could I** use your computer? 당신의 컴퓨터를 좀 사용해도 좋을까요?

〈긍정〉	〈부정〉
– Yes, you can(may).	– No, you can(may) not. 아니, 하면 안돼.
– Sure. / Certainly. / Of course. 물론이지	– No, please not.
– Why not? 왜 아냐?	– I'm sorry.
– Okay. / Go ahead. 그렇게 해.	

Tip! Could I ~/ May I ~는 Can I ~보다 정중한 표현이다.

3 must

🔷 의무 / 확신 : ~해야만 한다 / ~임에 틀림없다

ⓐ **긍정문**

〈의무〉 이 때 must는 have to, should로 바꾸어 쓸 수 있다.

ex. **We must leave now.** 우리는 지금 떠나야만 한다.

= We **have to** leave now.

= We **should** leave now.

〈확신〉 ex. **She must be a lawyer.** 그녀는 변호사임에 틀림없다.

ⓑ **부정문**

must, should, have to가 긍정문에서는 '~해야만 한다'로 그 뜻이 유사하지만, 부정문에서는 형태도 다르고 뜻도 다르다.

〈금지〉 must(should) not : ~해서는 안 된다.

ex. **You must(should) not play the game all day.**
너는 하루 종일 게임을 해서는 안된다.

〈불필요〉 don't have to : 할 필요가 없다.

ex. **You don't have to leave now.** 너는 지금 떠날 필요가 없다.

〈강한 부정적 추측〉 cannot be : ~일 리가 없다 (must~ : ~임에 틀림없다의 부정)

ex. **It cannot be true.** 그것은 사실일 리가 없다.

ⓒ **의문문**

〈의무〉 • Must 주어 ~? : ~해야만 하니?

ex. **Must I go now?** 내가 지금 가야만 하니?

– Yes, you must.

– No, you **don't have to.** 아니, 갈 필요 없어.

• Should 주어 ~? : ~해야만 하니?

ex. **Should I do it now?** 내가 지금 그것을 해야만 하니?

– Yes, you should.

– No, you should not.

• Do 주어 have to ~? : ~해야만 하니?

ex. **Do I have to go now?** 내가 지금 가야만 하니?

– Yes, you **have to.** (Yes, you do)

– No, you **don't have to.** (No, you don't)

1 조동사의 과거형과 미래형

1 can(능력)의 과거형과 미래형

can의 과거 : could. was / were able to ~할 수 있었다

can을 could로 바꿔 준다.

〈현재〉　*ex.* **He can drive a truck.** 그는 트럭을 운전할 수 있다.

〈과거〉　*ex.* **He could drive a truck.** 그는 트럭을 운전할 수 있었다.

can은 be able to로 바꿔 쓸 수 있으므로, 과거형은 was / were able to로 바꿔 쓸 수 있다.

〈현재〉　*ex.* **He is able to drive a truck.** 그는 트럭을 운전할 수 있다.

〈과거〉　*ex.* **He was able to drive a truck.** 그는 트럭을 운전할 수 있었다.

can의 미래 : will be able to ~할 수 있을 것이다

can의 미래형은 없으므로 be able to로 바꿔 이것의 미래형 will be able to를 쓰면 된다.

〈현재〉　*ex.* **He is able to run fast.** 그는 빨리 달릴 수 있다.

〈미래〉　*ex.* **He will be able to run fast.** 그는 빨리 달릴 수 있을 것이다.
~~He will can run fast.~~

현재	과거	미래
~할 수 있다	~할 수 있었다	~할 수 있을 것이다
can = am / are / is able to	could = was / were able to	will be able to

2 의무의 must/have to의 과거형과 미래형

과거 : had to ~해야만 했다

ⓐ **have to의 과거**

have (has) to는 had to로 바꿔 준다.

〈현재〉 *ex.* He has to study hard. 그는 열심히 공부해야만 한다.

〈과거〉 *ex.* He **had to** study hard. 그는 열심히 공부해야만 했다.

ⓑ **must의 과거**

must는 과거형이 없으므로 같은 뜻을 가진 have to의 과거형인 **had to**를 이용한다.

〈현재〉 *ex.* He must wait for one hour. 그는 한 시간 동안 기다려야만 한다.

〈과거〉 *ex.* He **had to** wait for one hour. 그는 한 시간동안 기다려야만 했다.

미래 : will have to ~해야만 할 것이다

ⓐ **have to의 미래**

have (has) to는 will have to로 바꿔 준다.

〈현재〉 *ex.* You have to excuse him. 너는 그에게 사과해야만 한다.

〈미래〉 *ex.* You **will have to** excuse him. 너는 그에게 사과해야만 할 것이다.

ⓑ **must의 미래**

must는 미래형이 없으므로 같은 뜻을 가진 have to의 미래형인 **will have to**를 이용한다.

〈현재〉 *ex.* You must return it. 너는 그것을 반납해야만 한다.

〈과거〉 *ex.* He **will have to** return it. 너는 그것을 반납해야만 할 것이다.

현재	과거	미래
~해야만 한다	~해야만 했다	~해야만 할 것이다
must, have / has to	had to	will have to

A 기초 TEST

정답 및 해설 **p.14**

다음 중 알맞은 것을 골라 보자.

1 can see   (**볼 수 있다,** 볼 수 있을 것이다, 볼 수 있었다)

    was able to see   (볼 수 있다, 볼 수 있을 것이다, 볼 수 있었다)

    could see   (볼 수 있다, 볼 수 있을 것이다, 볼 수 있었다)

    will be able to see   (볼 수 있다, 볼 수 있을 것이다, 볼 수 있었다)

2 will have to work   (일해야만 한다, 일해야만 할 것이다, 일해야만 했다)

    must work   (일해야만 한다, 일해야만 할 것이다, 일해야만 했다)

    had to work   (일해야만 한다, 일해야만 할 것이다, 일해야만 했다)

    has to work   (일해야만 한다, 일해야만 할 것이다, 일해야만 했다)

다음 중 알맞은 것을 골라 보자.

1 만들 수 있었다   (can, **could,** will be able to) make

    만들 수 있을 것이다   (can, could, will be able to) make

    만들 수 있다   (can, could, will be able to) make

    만들 수 있었다   (can, was/were able to, will be able to) make

2 떠나야만 할 것이다   (must, had to, will have to) leave

    떠나야만 한다   (must, had to, will have to) leave

    떠나야만 했다   (must, had to, will have to) leave

    떠나야만 한다   (have/has to, had to, will have to) leave

다음 주어진 문장의 과거형을 모두 골라 보자. (두 개 가능)

1 She can baby-sit your child today.
   → She (could, was able to, had to) baby-sit your child today.

2 We must organize a party for him.
   → We (must had to, should had to, had to) organize a party for him.

3 He has to walk from here to the subway station.
   → He (could, was able to, had to) walk from here to the subway station.

4 I have to wear a suit to his graduation.
   → I (must, could, had to) wear a suit to his graduation.

5 Can they jump over the fence?
   → (Were they able to, Were they able, Could they) jump over the fence?

다음 주어진 문장의 미래형을 골라 보자.

1 Jake can eat a whole steak in 3 minutes.
   → Jake (will be able to, will able to, will can) eat a whole steak in 3 minutes.

2 He must practice all day.
   → He (will must, will have to, will should) practice all day.

3 Amy has to read a book in one day.
   → Amy (will has to, will have to, will had to) read a book in one day.

4 I can fix my bike.
   → I (will able to, will be able to, will can) fix my bike.

5 She can make a reservation at the hotel.
   → She (will be able to, will can, will able to) make a reservation at the hotel.

organize 기획(조직)하다   make a reservation 예약하다

C 기초 TEST

정답 및 해설 p.14

다음 주어진 문장의 과거형을 만들어 보자.

1 Sam can pick the oranges.

→ Sam *could pick* the oranges.

→ Sam *was able to pick* the oranges

2 We must drive a car for about 10 miles.

→ We a car for about 10 miles.

3 She can make ramen.

→ She ramen.

→ She ramen.

4 He has to sow the seeds.

→ He the seeds.

5 She must speak quietly.

→ She quietly.

6 My dog can do a back-flip.

→ My dog a back-flip.

→ My dog a back-flip.

7 They are able to get tickets for the show.

→ They tickets for the show.

→ They tickets for the show.

8 I can make a bed before the guests arrive.

→ I a bed before the guests arrive.

→ I a bed before the guests arrive.

---

sow (씨)뿌리다   seed 씨   back-flip 뒤집기   make a bed 침대를 정리하다   guest 손님

A 기본 TEST

다음 주어진 문장의 미래형을 만들어 보자.

1 Sam can do it.

　→ Sam _____ *will be able to do* _____ it.

2 You must apologize to her.

　→ You _____ to her.

3 The child is able to use chopsticks very well.

　→ The child _____ chopsticks very well.

4 She must answer the question before time runs out.

　→ She _____ the question before time runs out.

5 We are able to do more.

　→ We _____ more.

6 I have to hear him.

　→ I _____ him.

7 She can do as much as you.

　→ She _____ as much as you.

8 You must keep an appointment.

　→ You _____ an appointment.

9 Laura can finish it before lunch break.

　→ Laura _____ it before lunch break.

10 Peter has to face the fact.

　→ Peter _____ the fact.

---

accept 받아들이다　**apologize** 사과하다　**noodle** 국수　**run out** 다 되다　**in time** 제시간에
keep an appointment 약속을 지키다　**lunch break** 점심 휴식 시간　**face** 대면하다, 마주하다

정답 및 해설 **p.15**

다음 주어진 문장을 지시대로 바꿔 써 보자.

1 You must get along with your neighbor. (미래)

→ *You will have to get* along with your neighbor.

2 She can care about her grade. (과거)

→ about her grade.

3 Carol must wear sun-block lotion at the beach. (과거)

→ sun-block lotion at the beach.

4 Ants have to work together. (미래)

→ together.

5 The tiger can catch a zebra. (미래)

→ a zebra.

6 She must keep the baby from crying. (과거)

→ the baby from crying.

7 You are able to do well on this test. (미래)

→ well on this test.

8 Tony is able to cut the cheese. (과거)

→ the cheese.

9 Nancy must wait in line. (과거)

→ in line.

10 The police can arrest him. (미래)

→ him.

---

care about ~에 대해 신경을 쓴다   **grade** 성적   **keep A from B** A가 B를 못하게 하다   **arrest** 체포하다

UNIT 2 조동사의 관용구

● had better + 동사원형 : ~하는 것(편)이 낫다 (강한 충고, 경고)

ex. **You had better do your homework first.** 너는 우선 숙제를 하는 것이 낫다.

● would rather + 동사원형 : (차라리) ~하는 편이 낫겠다.

ex. **You would rather stay at home.** 너는 차라리 집에 있는 편이 좋겠다.

* would rather 뒤에 비교하는 대상이 있을 때는 than을 사용한다.
ex. You **would rather** stay at home **than** go to school. 너는 학교에 가느니 차라리 집에 있는 편이 좋겠다.

● used to (would) + 동사원형 : ~하곤 했다 (과거의 습관)

더 이상 행하지 않는 과거의 습관을 말한다. → 이때는 **would**로 바꿔 쓸 수 있다.

ex. **He used to get up early.** 그는 일찍 일어나곤 했다.(지금은 안한다.)
　　 = **He would get up early.**

● used to + 동사원형 : ~이었다 (과거의 상태)

현재 계속되고 있지 않은 과거의 상태를 말한다. → 이때는 **would**로 바꿔 쓸 수 없다.

ex. **There used to be a tree around here.** (Now there isn't.)
　　 이 근처에 나무 한 그루가 있었다. (지금은 없다.)
　　 ~~There would be a tree around here.~~

● be used to + 동명사 : ~하는데 익숙하다

ex. **He is used to washing a car.** 그는 세차하는데 익숙하다.

● get used to + 동명사 : ~하는 데 익숙해지다

ex. **She got used to cooking fish.** 그녀는 생선 요리하는 데 익숙해졌다.

● may well + 동사원형 : ~하는 것은 당연하다

ex. **You may well say so.** 네가 그렇게 말하는 것은 당연하다.

● may as well + 동사원형 : ~하는 것이 좋겠다.

ex. **He may as well stay at home.** 그는 집에 있는 것이 좋겠다.

다음 중 보기에서 알맞은 것을 골라 연결해 보자.

> | 보기 |
>
> 1. ~하는 데 익숙해지다
> 2. ~하는 데 익숙하다
> 3. (차라리) ~하는 편이 낫겠다
> 4. ~하는 것(편)이 낫다
> 5. ~하는 것은 당연하다
> 6. ~이었다 (과거의 상태)
> 7. ~하곤 했다 (과거의 습관)
> 8. ~하는 것이 좋겠다

1 may as well + 동사 원형   *8*

2 would rather + 동사 원형

3 may well + 동사 원형

4 used to + 동사 원형

5 had better + 동사 원형

6 get used to ~ing

7 (be) used to ~ing

---

rather 오히려, 차라리

B 기초 TEST

다음 중 보기에서 알맞은 관용구를 골라 빈칸에 써 보자.

┌─ |보기| ─────────────────────────┐
│
│　　　used to + 동사 원형
│　　　(be) used to ~ing
│　　　get used to ~ing
│　　　may well + 동사 원형
│　　　may as well + 동사 원형
│　　　had better + 동사 원형
│　　　would rather + 동사 원형
│
└──────────────────────────────────┘

1 ～하곤 했다 (과거의 습관)　　　　　　　　*used to + 동사 원형*

2 ～이었다(과거의 상태)

3 ～하는 것은 당연하다

4 ～하는 것(편)이 낫다

5 (차라리) ～하는 편이 낫겠다

6 ～하는 데 익숙해지다

7 ～하는 데 익숙하다

8 ～하는 것이 좋겠다

다음 주어진 단어를 이용하여 우리말에 알맞게 문장을 완성해 보자.

1 Tommy는 그 개울을 따라 걷곤 했었다. (요즘은 걷지 않는다.)

Tommy *used to walk (would walk)* along the stream. (walk)

2 그는 그의 자동차를 닦는 데 익숙하다.

He his car. (wash)

3 그녀가 우는 것은 당연하다.

She . (cry)

4 그는 지금부터 기다리는데 익숙해질 것이다.

He'll from now on. (wait)

5 나는 차라리 집에서 쉬는 편이 낫겠다.

I a rest at home. (take)

6 이 거리에 카페가 하나 있었다. (지금은 없다.)

There a cafe on the street. (be)

7 우리는 서로 만나곤 했었다. (지금은 못 만난다.)

We each other. (see)

8 그들이 화가 나는 것은 당연하다.

They upset. (get)

9 지금 우리는 택시를 잡는 것이 낫다.

Now, we a taxi. (catch)

10 너는 차라리 벽한테 이야기 하는 편이 낫겠다.

You to the wall. (talk)

---

each other 서로   from now on 지금부터   cafe 카페

A 실력 TEST

주어진 문장을 참고하고, 알맞은 조동사 관용구와 ( ) 안의 단어를 사용하여 빈칸을 채워보자.

1 She played the cello before. But, now she doesn't.

→ She _____ *used to play (would play)* _____ the cello. (play)

2 Jane got fatter than last year. I think she should do the exercise.

→ She _____ m _____ the exercise. (do)

3 There was a bakery here. But, it is gone.

→ There _____ a bakery here. (be)

4 It is natural that Cathy should be proud of herself.

→ Cathy _____ proud of herself. (be)

5 Mrs. Lee has taught music for a long time.

→ Now she _____ is _____ music. (teach)

6 Jim has used my PC several times.

→ Jim _____ g _____ my PC. (use)

7 We cannot stay here. So, we are going to leave here.

→ We _____ here than stay. (leave)

8 You ate a lot. So, I think you should stop eating.

→ You _____ h _____ eating. (stop)

9 It is natural that the apple should turn red in fall.

→ The apple _____ red in fall. (turn)

10 We sometimes went hiking. But, now we don't.

→ Sometimes we _____ u _____ hiking. (go)

---

exercise 운동   natural 자연스러운   turn 바뀌다

[01~02] 지시대로 바꿔 보시오.

01

> Jim can understand it soon.

과거 _____

_____

미래 _____

02

> Sumi must do her homework.

과거 _____

미래 _____

03 두 문장이 같은 뜻이 되도록 빈칸에 알맞은 말을 고르시오.

> Tommy could move the stones alone.
> = Tommy _____ able to move the stones alone.

① is
② are
③ were
④ was
⑤ did

04 밑줄 친 부분이 바르지 않은 것을 고르시오.

① She had to go to Russia.
② They were able to help him.
③ He will able to carry the luggage.
④ Tom will have to leave here.
⑤ He had to learn more.

luggage 수하물

05 다음 우리말을 영어로 바르게 옮긴 것을 고르시오.

> 그는 그것에 대해 나에게 물어 봐야만 했다.

① He must to ask me about it.
② He will have to ask me about it.
③ He had to ask me about it.
④ He had asked to me about it.
⑤ He was able to ask me about it.

06 다음 중 바르게 쓰인 문장을 고르시오.

① Tony were able to come then.
② Jane coulds put it on.
③ Christie must keeps the promise.
④ You will have to meet her.
⑤ He had to gets up early.

07 ( ) 안의 단어를 사용하여 우리말에 맞게 영어로 써 넣으시오.

> 우리는 그 때 일하는 것을 멈춰만 했다. (stop)
>
> →We _____
>
> working at that time.

at that time 그 때, 그 당시에

08 다음 빈칸에 알맞은 말을 넣으시오.

> Tony는 혼자 할머니댁에 갈 수 있었다.
>
> →Tony _____
> go to grandmother's by himself.
>
> →Tony _____
> go to grandmother's by himself.

09 다음 빈칸에 공통으로 알맞은 말을 고르시오.

> • Jane will be able _____ eat a lemon.
> • I will have _____ do my homework.

① to
② in
③ of
④ on
⑤ with

10 아래의 문장과 밑줄 친 문장의 쓰임이 같지 않은 것을 고르시오.

> Joseph <u>could</u> play the violin.

① She could make a pineapple pizza.
② Could I use your pen?
③ Jenny could raise cows.
④ He could speak French.
⑤ I could find him.

French 프랑스어

[11-13] 우리말과 일치하도록 빈칸에 알맞은 말을 쓰시오.

11

나는 Jane을 태워 올 수 있었다.

I _____ pick up Jane.

12

우리는 3시까지 거기에 도착할 수 있을거야.

We _____ get there by 3.

13

그들은 비 때문에 텐트에서 잠을 자야만 할 것이다.

They _____ sleep in a tent because of rain.

14 다음 중 틀린 부분을 찾아 바르게 고쳐 보시오.

You had better taking off your hat.
너는 너의 모자를 벗는 게 낫겠다.

_____ → _____

15 다음 어법상 옳은 것을 고르면?

① He would rather asking her.
② She had better to drink ice water.
③ He may as well going to college.
④ Tom would cooking for his girlfriend.
⑤ She is used to selecting color.

select 선택(발)하다

16 밑줄 친 말과 바꾸어 쓸 수 있는 것을 고르시오.

I was able to speak English.

① should
② would
③ must
④ could
⑤ was

[17–18] 다음 글을 읽고 물음에 답하시오.

ⓐ Karen had to taking care of her little brother. But she wanted to go to Tony's party. So, Karen went to the party with her little brother. Everyone enjoyed the party. But Karen's parents were worried about their kids, because Karen didn't leave a message for them. Karen ⓑ _____ leave a message next time.

Karen은 다음 번에는 메세지를 남겨놔야만 할 것이다.

17 밑줄 친 ⓐ에서 틀린 부분을 찾아 바르게 고치시오.

_____ → _____

18 밑줄 친 ⓑ에 들어갈 말을 우리말에 맞게 고르시오.

① will must
② will have to
③ had to
④ will has to
⑤ have to

[19–20] 주어진 단어를 이용하여 우리말과 일치하도록 빈칸에 알맞은 말을 쓰시오.

19

This soup tastes flat. So, I think you should put some salt in it.

= You _____ some salt in the soup. (may, put)

너는 수프에 약간의 소금을 넣는 것이 좋겠다.

flat (음식이) 맛없는

20

He has eaten nothing since yesterday.

He _____ hungry. (be)

그는 배고픈 것이 당연하다.

since yesterday 어제 부터

01 다음 조동사의 과거 형태가 바르게 연결되지 않은 것을 고르시오.

① can - could
② is able to - was able to
③ must - might
④ are able to – were able to
⑤ has to - had to

02 다음 밑줄 친 조동사와 바꿔 쓸 수 있는 것을 고르시오.

He could not speak in English.

① cannot
② would not
③ was not able to
④ were not able to
⑤ had not to

03 다음 밑줄 친 조동사 중 나머지 하나와 의미가 다른 것을 고르시오.

① I must wake up early.
② He should pay his debt.
③ She has to answer the phone.
④ We have to work hard.
⑤ You may play outside.

04 다음 문장에서 밑줄 친 부분을 바르게 고치시오.

She will can do the job.
그녀는 그 일을 할 수 있을 것이다.

will can → _____

05 다음 문장을 우리말로 바르게 옮긴 것은?

He will have to ask her forgiveness.

① 그는 그녀에게 용서를 구해야만 했다.
② 그는 그녀에게 용서를 구한다.
③ 그는 그녀에게 용서를 구할 것이다.
④ 그는 그녀에게 용서를 구해야 할 것이다.
⑤ 그는 그녀를 용서해야만 했다.

forgiveness 용서

06 다음 문장을 과거형으로 바르게 옮긴 것을 고르시오.

We must listen carefully to the teacher.

① We should listen carefully to the teacher.
② We had to listen carefully to the teacher.
③ We has to listen carefully to the teacher.
④ We have to listen carefully to the teacher.
⑤ We did must listen carefully to the teacher.

07 다음 문장을 미래형으로 바르게 옮긴 것을 고르시오.

> She can play the violin well.

① She will can play the violin well.
② She will able to play the violin well.
③ She will be able to play the violin well.
④ She will be able play the violin well.
⑤ She can will play the violin well.

08 다음 우리말에 맞게 빈칸에 들어갈 말을 고르시오.

> You _____ go to the hospital
> than take the class.
> 너는 수업을 듣느니 차라리 병원에 가는 것이 낫겠다.

① would rather
② had rather
③ had to
④ may well
⑤ may as well

09 다음 우리말에 맞게 빈칸에 들어갈 말을 고르시오.

> You will _____ getting
> up early.
> 너는 일찍 일어나는 것에 익숙해질 것이다.

① may well
② may as well
③ use to
④ used to
⑤ get used to

10 다음 밑줄 친 부분 중 would로 바꿔 쓸 수 없는 문장을 고르시오.

① There used to be a bakery at the corner.
② I used to study at the library.
③ She often used to take subway.
④ We used to walk the dog.
⑤ The family used to eat out.

11 다음 밑줄 친 부분이 어색한 것을 고르시오.

① You may well be angry with her.
② You had better sleep more.
③ He would rather stay at home.
④ I am used to cook Ramyen.
⑤ We may as well take a break.

Ramyen 라면

12 다음 중 어법상 틀린 것을 고르시오.

> When I was a kid, I often used to
> ① wake up while ② sleeping.
> As I ③ grew up, I got ④ used to
> ⑤ sleep without parents.

13 다음 ( )안의 말을 사용하여 우리말에 맞게 빈칸을 채우시오.

> 그가 그녀를 좋아하는 것은 당연하다.
> He _____ _____ _____ her.
> (may)

[14-15] 다음 대화를 읽고 물음에 답하시오.

> Boss : Welcome to the company.
> Sean : Thank you for hiring me.
> Boss : You're welcome. Do you have any question?
> Sean : ⓐ _____ I clean my office?
> Boss : Yes, you must. There is no cleaning service yet.
> Sean : I understand.
> Boss : You ⓑ(used, your, will, work, to, get, doing).

14 ⓐ에 들어갈 수 있는 조동사를 적으시오.

ⓐ : _____

15 ⓑ의 단어를 바르게 배열하시오.

You ⓑ _____

16 다음 중 바르게 쓰인 문장을 고르시오.

① Sam was finally able to finish the work.
② Jane could able to sell her old clothes.
③ Chris must keeps his promises.
④ He will has to meet my sister.
⑤ She had to gets up early.

[17–18] 다음 문장을 주어진 지시대로 바꾸어 쓰시오.

> He can understand his girlfriend.

17 He _____ his girlfriend. (과거)

18 He _____ his girlfriend. (미래)

19 다음 빈칸에 공통으로 알맞은 말을 고르시오.

> • He had _____ take care of his brother.
> • Blair and I used _____ play basketball.

① to
② in
③ of
④ on
⑤ with

20 다음 밑줄 친 조동사의 쓰임이 올바르지 <u>않은</u> 것을 고르시오.

① He <u>is able to</u> make a sandwich.
② I <u>had to</u> borrow her pen.
③ She <u>will able to</u> raise a cat.
④ It <u>may</u> be windy tomorrow morning.
⑤ You <u>should</u> help him.

Chapter 6

수동태

현재 / 과거 / 미래의 수동태

🔷 수동태의 모양 : 시제에 따라 'be동사'만 달라진다.

현재	am / are / is + 과거분사 (P.P)	~되어지다
과거	was / were + 과거분사 (P.P)	~되어졌다
미래	will be + 과거분사 (P.P)	~되어 질 것이다

〈현재〉 *ex.* My dad   fixes the car.
→ The car is fixed by my dad. 그 차는 나의 아빠에 의해 고쳐진다.

〈과거〉 *ex.* My dad   fixed the car.
→ The car was fixed by my dad. 그 차는 나의 아빠에 의해 고쳐졌다.

〈미래〉 *ex.* My dad   will fix the car.
→ The car will be fixed by my dad. 그 차는 나의 아빠에 의해 고쳐질 것이다.

A 기초 TEST

정답 및 해설 **p.16**

다음 중 알맞은 것을 골라 보자.

1 Some roses **were grown**.　　약간의 장미들이 (길러진다, 길러졌다, 길러질 것이다)

Some roses **are grown**.　　약간의 장미들이 (길러진다, 길러졌다, 길러질 것이다)

Some roses **will be grown**.　　약간의 장미들이 (길러진다, 길러졌다, 길러질 것이다)

2 The cookies **will be baked**.　　과자들이 (구워진다, 구워졌다, 구워질 것이다)

The cookies **are baked**.　　과자들이 (구워진다, 구워졌다, 구워질 것이다)

The cookies **were baked**.　　과자들이 (구워진다, 구워졌다, 구워질 것이다)

다음 중 알맞은 것을 골라 보자.

1 그 문은 나에 의해 칠해질 것이다.　　The door (is, was, will be) painted by me.

그 문은 나에 의해 칠해졌다.　　The door (is, was, will be) painted by me.

그 문은 나에 의해 칠해진다.　　The door (is, was, will be) painted by me.

2 그 뉴스는 Jim에 의해 보고되었다.　　The news (is, was, will be) reported by Jim.

그 뉴스는 Jim에 의해 보고된다.　　The news (is, was, will be) reported by Jim.

그 뉴스는 Jim에 의해 보고 되어질 것이다.　　The news (is, was, will be) reported by Jim.

3 뒷마당은 그에 의해 (낙엽이) 긁어 모아진다.　　The backyard (is, was, will be) raked by him.

뒷마당은 그에 의해 (낙엽이) 긁어 모아졌다.　　The backyard (is, was, will be) raked by him.

뒷마당은 그에 의해 (낙엽이) 긁어 모아질 것이다.　　The backyard (is, was, will be) raked by him.

---

report 보고하다　　**rake** 긁어 모으다

Chapter 6 159

다음 중 알맞은 것을 골라 보자.

1 The police (was called , will be called) by Jack.

경찰은 Jack에 의해 불리워졌다.

2 A lot of money (will be counted, was counted) by the cashier.

많은 돈이 계산원에 의해 세어질 것이다.

3 My sneakers (are washed, will be washed) once a week.

나의 운동화는 일주일에 한 번 세탁되어진다.

4 The jewelry store (is robbed, was robbed) 2 day ago.

그 보석가게는 이틀 전에 강도를 당했다.

5 Some vegetables (are soaked, were soaked) in the icy water for 30 minutes.

약간의 야채들이 30분 동안 얼음물에 담가져 있었다.

6 Her choice (is changed, will be changed) by her friend's advice.

그녀의 선택은 그녀의 친구의 충고에 의해 바뀌어 질 것이다.

7 A lot of animals (are rescued, were rescued) by Ben.

많은 동물들이 Ben에 의해 구조되었다.

8 His finger (was cut, is cut) by the sharp knife badly.

그의 손가락은 날카로운 칼에 의해 심하게 베었다.

9 The world cup soccer games (are televised, will be televised) live.

월드컵 축구 경기들이 텔레비전으로 생방송될 것이다.

10 The meeting (will be scheduled, is scheduled) next week.

그 회의는 다음 주로 예정되어 있다.

---

jewelry store 보석가게   rob 강탈하다   soak 담그다   televise 텔레비전으로 방송하다
schedule 스케줄을 짜다

C 기초 TEST

정답 및 해설 p.16

다음 주어진 문장의 시제를 고르고 수동태 문장으로 만들어 보자.

1 Linda made best tasting coffee.　(현재, 과거, 미래)

→ Best tasting coffee　*was made*　by Linda.

Linda will make best tasting coffee.　(현재, 과거, 미래)

→ Best tasting coffee　by Linda.

Linda makes best tasting coffee.　(현재, 과거, 미래)

→ Best tasting coffee　by Linda.

2 I will invite my best friend.　(현재, 과거, 미래)

→ My best friend　by me.

I invited my best friend.　(현재, 과거, 미래)

→ My best friend　by me.

I invite my best friend.　(현재, 과거, 미래)

→ My best friend　by me.

3 She saw the tall building.　(현재, 과거, 미래)

→ The tall building　by her.

She sees the tall building.　(현재, 과거, 미래)

→ The tall building　by her.

She will see the tall building.　(현재, 과거, 미래)

→ The tall building　by her.

best tasting coffee 최고의 맛이 나는 커피

다음 주어진 문장의 동사에 O표 한 후, 수동태 문장으로 만들어 보자.

1 He (designed) this watch.

→ This watch *was designed* by him.

2 The bride will throw the bouquet.

→ The bouquet by the bride.

3 The teacher solved the problems.

→ The problems by the teacher.

4 The mother comforts the baby.

→ The baby by the mother.

5 He removed the gloves.

→ The gloves by him.

6 Dolphins hunt seals.

→ Seals by dolphins.

7 They will shovel snow today.

→ Snow by them today.

8 The adult separated the fighting kids.

→ The fighting kids by the adult.

9 The movie touched a lot of people.

→ A lot of people by the movie.

10 The magician's trick will amaze us.

→ We by the magician's trick.

---

design 디자인하다 bride 신부 throw 던지다 (throw-threw-thrown) bouquet 부케
comfort 위로하다, 달래다 remove 제거하다 dolphin 돌고래 seal 물개 shovel 삽질하다 adult 어른
separate 분리하다 touch 감동시키다 magician 마술사 trick 속임수

다음 주어진 문장의 동사에 ○표 한 후, 수동태 문장으로 만들어 보자.

1　She will make ice cream.

　　→ Ice cream　　　　*will be made*　　　　by her.

2　His aunt sells chocolate.

　　→ Chocolate　　　　　　　　　　by his aunt.

3　She hangs up the phone.

　　→ The phone　　　　　　　　　　by her.

4　I folded the blanket.

　　→ The blanket　　　　　　　　　　by me.

5　Sara will knit a sweater.

　　→ A sweater　　　　　　　　　　by Sara.

6　Mary opened the curtain

　　→ The curtain　　　　　　　　　　by Mary.

7　He received two letters.

　　→ Two letters　　　　　　　　　　by him.

8　I will select a book.

　　→ A book　　　　　　　　　　by me.

9　A bee stung his hand.

　　→ His hand　　　　　　　　　　by a bee.

10　Jack polished the shoes.

　　→ The shoes　　　　　　　　　　by Jack.

---

fold 접다　　**knit** 짜다　　**select** 고르다　　**sting** 쏘다, 찌르다 (sting-stung-stung)　　**polish** 광을 내다

UNIT

2

조동사 / 진행형 / 현재완료의 수동태

💠 사이에 들어가는 'be동사의 형태'만 다르다.

조동사 수동태	조동사 + be + p.p	~되어져 + (조동사의 뜻)
진행형 수동태	be동사 + being + p.p	~되어지는 중이다
현재완료 수동태	have (has) + been + p.p	~되어졌다

〈조동사〉   *ex.* She   **must send** the letter.

     → The letter **must** | be | sent by her. 그 편지는 그녀에 의해 보내져야만 한다.

〈진행형〉   *ex.* My friends **are playing** the music.

     The music **is** | being | played by my friends.

     음악이 나의 친구들에 의해서 연주되어 지고 있는 중이다.

〈현재완료〉   *ex.* Tom   **has finished** this project.

     → This project **has** | been | finished by Tom. 이 프로젝트는 Tom에 의해서 끝마쳐졌다.

다음 중 우리말에 알맞은 것을 골라 보자.

1 The robot can be made.

그 로봇은 (만들어질 수 있다, 만들어져야 한다, 만들어질지도 모른다)

The robot may be made.

그 로봇은 (만들어질 수 있다, 만들어져야 한다, 만들어질지도 모른다)

The robot must be made.

그 로봇은 (만들어질 수 있다, 만들어져야 한다, 만들어질지도 모른다)

2 The bread is being toasted.

빵이 (구워지고 있는 중이다, 구워지고 있는 중이었다, 다 구워 졌다)

The bread was being toasted.

빵이 (구워지고 있는 중이다, 구워지고 있는 중이었다, 다 구워 졌다)

The bread has been toasted.

빵이 (구워지고 있는 중이다, 구워지고 있는 중이었다, 다 구워 졌다)

다음 중 영어로 알맞은 것을 골라 보자.

1 그 도둑이 경찰관에 의해 추적당하고 있다.

The thief (is being chased, are being chased, was being chased) by the police.

그 도둑이 경찰관에 의해 추적당할지도 모른다.

The thief (can be chased, may be chased, must be chased) by the police.

그 도둑이 경찰관에 의해 추적당한 적이 있다.

The thief (has been chased, are being chased, have been chased) by the police.

2 그 책은 출판되었다.

The book (is be published, must be published, has been published).

그 책은 출판되어야만 한다.

The book (is be published, must be published, has been published).

---

publish 출판하다   chase 추적하다

다음 중 알맞은 것을 골라 보자.

1 A pizza (may been delivered, (may be delivered)) by Tom.

피자가 Tom에 의해서 배달될 지도 모른다.

2 The movie (is been produced, is being produced) by some young people.

그 영화는 몇몇 젊은이들에 의해 제작되고 있는 중이다.

3 The code (has been erased, has being erased) by Jane.

암호가 Jane에 의해서 지워져 버렸다.

4 The lion (must be helped, may be helped) by the mouse.

그 사자는 그 생쥐에 의해 도움을 받을지도 모른다.

5 Bananas (have being eaten, have been eaten) by monkeys.

바나나가 원숭이들에 의해 다 먹혀졌다.

6 The leftover (can be packed, can being packed) by the waitress.

남은 음식은 그 직원에 의해서 포장되어 질 수 있다.

7 The cello (is being played, is be playing) by Jim.

첼로가 Jim에 의해서 연주되어 지고 있는 중이다.

8 Jason (has being moved, has been moved) by her art collection.

Jason은 그녀의 예술 수집품에 감동 받은 적이 있다.

9 The musical (was been performed, was being performed) by them.

그 뮤지컬은 그들에 의해서 공연되고 있던 중이었다.

10 This medicine (has to be taken, has to been taken) by grandma.

이 약은 할머니에 의해서 복용되어야만 한다.

---

deliver 배달하다   **erase** 지우다   **pack** 포장하다   **perform** 공연하다

B 기본 TEST

정답 및 해설 p.17

동사의 시제를 고르고 수동태 문장으로 만들어 보자.

1 Jimmy must cook dinner.

(조동사, 진행형, 현재완료)

→ Dinner *must be cooked* by Jimmy.

Jimmy is cooking dinner.

(조동사, 진행형, 현재완료)

→ Dinner by Jimmy.

Jimmy has cooked dinner.

(조동사, 진행형, 현재완료)

→ Dinner by Jimmy.

2 The tuner was tuning the piano.

(조동사, 진행형, 현재완료)

→ The piano by the tuner.

The tuner has tuned the piano.

(조동사, 진행형, 현재완료)

→ The piano by the tuner.

The tuner must tune the piano.

(조동사, 진행형, 현재완료)

→ The piano by the tuner.

3 Tom and Jane are making some sandwiches.

(조동사, 진행형, 현재완료)

→ Some sandwiches by Tom and Jane.

Tom and Jane have made some sandwiches.

(조동사, 진행형, 현재완료)

→ Some sandwiches by Tom and Jane.

Tom and Jane may make some sandwiches.

(조동사, 진행형, 현재완료)

→ Some sandwiches by Tom and Jane.

---

tune 조율하다

실력 TEST

동사에 ○표 한 후, 수동태 문장으로 만들어 보자.

1 Jane (is keeping) a pet.

→ A pet _is being kept_ by Jane.

2 Tom can hit a ball.

→ A ball by Tom.

3 I have done the project.

→ The project by me.

4 Ann can win the game.

→ The game by Ann.

5 The technician is repairing my smartphone.

→ My smartphone by the technician.

6 Mary must weed the garden.

→ The garden by Mary.

7 I have drilled a hole.

→ A hole by me.

8 We are sweeping the floor.

→ The floor by us.

9 He must send an e-mail.

→ An e-mail by him.

10 They have built the tower.

→ The tower by them.

---

technician 기술자, 기사   **weed** 잡초를 뽑다   **sweep** 쓸다 (sweep–swept–swept)

동사에 ○표 한 후, 수동태 문장으로 만들어 보자.

1 She may remember your face.

→ Your face   *may be remembered*   by her.

2 A mosquito has bitten him.

→ He   by a mosquito.

3 She is writing a poem.

→ A poem   by her.

4 He can break the promise.

→ The promise   by him.

5 They have built the bridge.

→ The bridge   by them.

6 Jane was grilling the pork ribs.

→ The pork ribs   by Jane.

7 Children should read this book.

→ This book   by Children.

8 My daughter is cutting the cake.

→ The cake   by my daughter.

9 Tom and Sara were singing the song.

→ The song   by Tom and Sara.

10 You have to take vitamins.

→ Vitamins   by you.

bite 물다   vitamin 비타민

1 4형식 문장의 수동태

4형식 문장은 목적어가 2개이므로 2가지 형태로 수동태를 만들 수 있다.

🔷 간접목적어를 주어로 하는 경우

간접목적어를 주어로 만든 다음, 직접목적어는 그대로 두고, 수동태로 만들면 된다.

ex. He gave **me** a pen.

→ **I** was given a pen by him. 나는 그에 의해서 펜이 주어졌다.

🔷 직접목적어를 주어로 하는 경우

직접목적어를 주어로 만든 다음, 간접목적어는 그대로 두고, 수동태로 만들면 된다.

이 때 간접 목적어 앞에 전치사를 붙여줘야 한다.

ex. He gave me **a pen**.

→ **A pen** was given **to** me by him. 펜이 그에 의해서 나에게 주어졌다.

ex. He made me **a kite**.

→ **A kite** was made **for** me by him. 연이 그에 의해서 나를 위하여 만들어졌다.

ex. She asked him **a question**.

→ **A question** was asked **of** him by her. 질문 하나가 그녀에 의해 그에게 질문되어졌다.

동사에 따른 간접 목적어 앞에 전치사

to 를 사용하는 동사	give, show, teach, tell, send, pass, read, write
for 를 사용하는 동사	make, cook, buy, find
of 를 사용하는 동사	ask

간접목적어를 주어로 하여 수동태 문장을 만들지 않는 동사들이 있다.

ex. He made his son a kite.

→ ~~His son was made a kite by him.~~ 그의 아들이 그에 의해 연으로 만들어 졌다?

→ A kite was made for his son by him.

직접목적어만을 주어로 쓰는 동사

make, cook, buy, send, pass, read, write....

2 5형식 문장의 수동태

🔷 5형식 문장은 목적어와 보어 중 '목적어'만 수동태의 주어로 하여 수동태를 만들 수 있다.

보어는 그대로 두고 목적어를 수동태의 주어로 하여 만들면 된다.

ex. She called him Brian.
　　　　　　　목적어　목적보어

　→ **He** was called Brian by her. 그는 그녀에 의해서 Brian이라고 불리어졌다.

5형식에서 목적보어가 명사일 경우 목적어로 착각하여 문장의 주어로 만들지 않도록 주의 한다.

ex. She called him Brian.
　　　　　　　목적어　　보어(명사)

　→ **He** was called Brian by her. 그는 그녀에 의해서 Brian이라고 불리어졌다.

　→ ~~Brian was called him by her.~~ Brian이 그녀에 의해서 그를이라고 불렸다?

🔷 원형부정사의 수동태

　ⓐ 지각동사의 목적보어로 쓰인 원형부정사는 to부정사로 바꿔 준다.

　　ex. I saw him **go** out. 나는 그가 외출하는 것을 보았다.

　　　→ He was seen **to go** out by me.

　ⓑ 사역동사(make, help) 의 목적보어로 쓰인 원형부정사도 to부정사로 바꿔 준다.

　　ex. She made him **paint** his room. 그녀는 그가 그의 방을 칠하도록 시켰다.

　　　→ He was made **to paint** his room by her.

　　단, 사역동사 have는 수동태로 만들 수 없다.

기초 TEST

다음 문장에서 간접목적어를 찾아 ○표 하고 수동태로 만들어 보자.

1 She gave (him) a sweater.

→ *He* _____ *was given* _____ *a sweater* _____ by her.

2 Tom gave me a pen.

→ _____ _____ _____ by Tom.

3 Liz showed them a necklace.

→ _____ _____ _____ by Liz.

4 He teaches us P.E.

→ _____ _____ _____ by him.

5 Eli told me her love story.

→ _____ _____ _____ by Eli.

다음 문장에서 직접목적어를 찾아 ○표 하고 수동태로 만들어 보자.

1 Dad cooked us (pork).

→ *Pork* _____ *was cooked* _____ for _____ *us* _____ by dad.

2 Bill sends us some cookies.

→ _____ _____ to _____ by Bill.

3 The teacher will write Paul a memo.

→ _____ _____ to _____ by the teacher.

4 She reads me a story book.

→ _____ _____ to _____ by her.

5 Ann passed Tom a ruler.

→ _____ _____ to _____ by Ann.

show 보여주다 (show - showed - shown)   P.E. 체육   memo 메모   ruler 자

다음 중 알맞은 것을 골라 보자.

1 A doll was given (to , for, of) me by him.

2 The salt was passed (to, for, of) me by Jake.

3 Science will be taught (to, for, of) them by Mr. Green.

4 Some chocolate are sent (to, for, of) them by her.

5 The story was told (to, for, of) his son by him.

6 A pinwheel was made (to, for, of) his niece by uncle.

7 A bundle of flowers was given (to, for, of) her by Tom.

8 The ring will be shown (to, for, of) him by Sally.

9 A muffler was bought (to, for, of) Paul by her.

10 Curry and rice is cooked (to, for, of) her sons by mom.

11 A message will be sent (to, for, of) her friends by Kate.

12 Some water was given (to, for, of) us by him.

13 A scarf will be bought (to, for, of) Ann by Jim.

14 Art is taught (to, for, of) us by him.

15 A lot of questions were asked (to, for, of) him by her.

pinwheel 바람개비   **muffler** 머플러   **scarf** 스카프

다음 주어진 문장을 수동태 문장으로 만들어 보자.

1 He gave me a pen.

→ I   *was given*   *a pen*   *by him*

→ A pen   *was given*   *to me*   *by him*

2 She teaches us math.

→ We

→ Math

3 She passed him her notebook.

→ Her notebook

4 My auntie made me a paper rose.

→ A paper rose

5 Jane will show him her painting.

→ He

→ Her painting

6 He bought her a big bag.

→ A big bag

7 Jimmy gave them some food.

→ They

→ Some food

8 Mom cooked us noodle.

→ Noodle

---

auntie 고모, 이모   **paper rose** 종이장미   **noodle** 국수

기본 TEST

정답 및 해설 p.18

다음 문장에서 목적어를 찾아 ○표 하고 수동태로 만들어 보자.

1 She made (her son) a musician.

→ *Her son* _____*was made*_____ _____*a musician*_____ by her.

2 They named the baby Sally.

→ _____ _____ by them.

3 We call the river 'Han-kang'.

→ _____ _____ by us.

4 I believe him generous.

→ _____ _____ by me.

5 Jimmy painted the ceiling white.

→ _____ _____ by Jimmy.

다음 문장에서 목적어를 찾아 ○표 하고 수동태로 만들어 보자.

1 I saw (him) enter the house.

→ *He* _____*was seen*_____ _____*to enter the house*_____ by me.

2 We heard her come closer.

→ _____ _____ by us.

3 She made him do his homework.

→ _____ _____ by her.

4 James helps his brother do the laundry work.

→ _____ _____ by James.

5 They make him act like a gentleman.

→ _____ _____ by them.

musician 음악가   closer 더 가까이   do the laundry work 세탁일을 하다

Chapter 6 175

C 기본 TEST

다음 문장에서 목적어를 찾아 O표 하고 수동태로 만들어 보자.

1 The girl colored (the board) green.

→ *The board* _____*was colored*_____ _____*green*_____ _____*by the girl*_____ .

2 They call the sea 'the Pacific'.

→ _____ _____ _____ .

3 The teacher makes us write a book report.

→ _____ _____ _____ .

4 The assigment made him tired.

→ _____ _____ _____ .

5 Bob found the story false.

→ _____ _____ _____ .

6 Jane felt the wind blow hard.

→ _____ _____ _____ .

7 Americans elected Obama President.

→ _____ _____ _____ .

8 She makes him upset.

→ _____ _____ _____ .

9 Dad helps me to finish work.

→ _____ _____ _____ .

10 Brian and Kate named the kitten 'Ming-Ming'.

→ _____ _____ _____ .

---

the Pacific 태평양   book report 독후감   false 거짓의

D 기본 TEST

정답 및 해설 **p.18, 19**

다음 문장에서 목적어를 찾아 ○표 하고 수동태로 만들어 보자.

1 She made (him) stop it.

→ _He_ _____was made_____ _____to stop it_____ _____by her_____ .

2 She considers him a professor.

→ _____ _____ _____ .

3 I bought him a trendy tie.

→ _____ _____ _____ .

4 They helped her to escape.

→ _____ _____ _____ .

5 Tom left the door open.

→ _____ _____ _____ .

6 She found Paul good.

→ _____ _____ _____ .

7 We made her cry.

→ _____ _____ _____ .

8 Jenny saw students study in the library.

→ _____ _____ _____ .

9 The news made him sad.

→ _____ _____ _____ .

10 We found the man homeless.

→ _____ _____ _____ .

professor 교수   **trendy** 유행하는   **escape** 탈출하다   **homeless** 집이 없는

UNIT 4

by 이외의 전치사를 사용하는 수동태

⬥ by 대신 with를 쓰는 동사

be covered with ~	~로 덮여있다
be pleased with(at) ~	~로 즐겁다
be satisfied with ~	~에 만족하다
be crowded with ~	~로 붐비다
be filled with ~	~로 가득 차다
be tired with ~	~로 피곤하다

ex. **This bottle is filled with cold water.** 이 병은 찬물로 가득 차 있다.

⬥ by 대신 of를 쓰는 동사

be tired of ~	~에 싫증나다
be made of / from~	~로 만들어지다

Tip!
be made of~ : 물리적 변화
be made from~ : 화학적 변화

⬥ by 대신 in을 쓰는 동사

be interested in ~	~에 흥미가 있다
be involved in ~	~에 관련(연관)되다

⬥ by 대신 at을 쓰는 동사

be surprised at (by) ~	~에 놀라다
be disappointed at ~	~에 실망하다

⬥ by 대신 to / about를 쓰는 동사

be known to ~	~에게 알려지다
be worried about ~	~에 대해 걱정하다

보기에서 알맞은 것을 골라 보자.

| 보기 |

| with | at | of / from | about | in | to | at (by) |

1	~로 즐겁다	be pleased	*with / at*	~
2	~에 흥미가 있다	be interested		~
3	~로 피곤하다	be tired		~
4	~로 붐비다	be crowded		~
5	~에 만족하다	be satisfied		~
6	~에게 알려지다	be known		~
7	~로 덮혀 있다	be covered		~
8	~에 놀라다	be surprised		~
9	~로 가득 차다	be filled		~
10	~에 싫증나다	be tired		~
11	~에 대해 걱정하다	be worried		~
12	~로 만들어지다	be made		~
13	~에 실망하다	be disappointed		~
14	~에 관련(연관)되다	be involved		~

A 기본 TEST

1 We are satisfied _with_ our house.

2 The ground is covered _____ mud.

3 Dad is worried _____ his company.

4 I am interested _____ chess.

5 The plaza is crowed _____ a lot of young people.

6 I am tired _____ listening to the song.

7 We all were surprised _____ the idea.

8 The boy is known _____ all students.

9 They are disappointed _____ the result.

10 Frank is pleased _____ the present.

11 The bottle is filled _____ oil.

12 Paper is made _____ wood.

13 I am tired _____ doing chores.

14 Tom is involved _____ the matter.

---

mud 진흙　　company 회사　　chess 체스　　result 결과　　chores (집안의) 잡다한 일　　involve 연관되다
matter 사건, 일

우리말에 알맞게 문장을 완성해 보자.

1 He _isn't interested in_ K-pop.

그는 K-pop에 관심이 없다.

2 We the number of her shoes.

우리는 그녀의 신발 개수에 놀랐다.

3 The baby the toy.

그 아기는 그 장난감에 싫증이 났다.

4 She her daughter's safety.

그녀는 그녀의 딸의 안전에 대해 걱정했다.

5 I my present situation.

나는 나의 현재 상황에 만족한다.

6 Jessy doing her housework.

Jessy는 그녀의 집안일로 피곤하다.

7 Plastics petroleum.

플라스틱은 석유로 만들어졌다.

8 The kitchen smoke.

부엌이 연기로 가득 차 있다.

9 Sausages pork.

소시지는 돼지고기로 만들어진다.

10 Mom my grade.

엄마는 내 성적에 실망하고 있다.

---

safety 안전 **present** 현재 **situation** 상황 **plastic** 플라스틱 **petroleum** 석유 **smoke** 연기

우리말에 알맞게 문장을 완성해 보자.

1 This drug store _is crowded with_ patients always.

그 약국은 항상 환자들로 붐빈다

2 Her name the whole world.

그녀의 이름은 전 세계에 알려져 있다.

3 The road snow.

길이 눈으로 덮여있다.

4 My heart love for her.

나의 심장은 그녀에 대한 사랑으로 가득차 있다.

5 I don't want to that.

나는 그 일에 연관되기를 원치 않는다.

6 They winning the game.

그들은 게임에 이긴 것을 기뻐하고 있다.

7 Young people their future.

젊은이들은 그들의 미래에 대해 걱정하고 있다.

8 Jake math.

Jake은 수학에 관심이 있다.

9 This furniture steel.

이 가구는 강철로 만들어졌다.

10 All of us her rudeness.

우리 모두는 그녀의 무례함에 놀랐다.

---

drug store 약국   patient 환자   the whole world 전 세계   heart 심장   steel 강철   rudeness 무례함

[01–03] 두 문장이 같은 뜻이 되도록 빈칸에 알맞은 말을 고르시오.

01

She writes an essay.
= An essay _____ by her.

① is wrote
② is written
③ does wrote
④ does written
⑤ be written

essay 수필

02

Her son broke the window.
= The window _____ by her son.

① was broke
② did broken
③ did broke
④ was broken
⑤ be broken

03

He will buy a shirt.
= A shirt _____ by him.

① will be buying
② will bought
③ will be bought
④ will do bought
⑤ be bought

04 우리말에 맞도록 ( ) 안의 단어를 알맞게 배열하시오.

그 집은 아빠에 의해 만들어 지고 있는 중이다.
(the house, by, being, built, dad, is)

→ The house _____

_____ .

05 다음 문장에서 **틀린** 것을 고르시오.

It ① should ② been ③ done
④ by ⑤ him.
그것은 그에 의해서 마무리되어야 한다.

06 다음을 수동태로 바꾸었을 때 빈칸에 들어갈 말을 써 넣으시오.

My teacher has ended the class.
→ The class has _____
ended by my teacher.

07 다음 중 어법상 <u>어색한</u> 것을 고르시오.

① These flowers will be sent to Jane.
② My car was stolen last month.
③ The bus was being checking by her.
④ The book has been returned by Andy.
⑤ The salary can be paid by him.

08 다음 문장을 수동태로 바꾸었을 때 빈칸에 알맞은 말을 고르시오.

My sister gave me a doll.
→ A doll was given _____ by my sister.

① me
② to me
③ of me
④ for me
⑤ at me

09 다음 문장을 2가지 형태의 수동태로 바꿀 때, 옳지 <u>않은</u> 부분을 고르시오.

Emma gave him this cap.
→ He ① was given ② to this cap by Emma.
→ ③ This cap ④ was given ⑤ to him by Emma.

10 다음 중 바르지 <u>않은</u> 문장을 고르시오.

① The skirt was made for me by Jenny.
② A message was sent to Kate by Jane.
③ The story was read to us by the teacher.
④ Tommy was bought the book by him
⑤ Kelly was elected captain by us.

11 다음 빈칸에 알맞은 것을 고르시오.

> The famous tree ＿＿＿＿＿＿
> here.

① can is seen
② can been seen
③ can have seen
④ can being seen
⑤ can be seen

12 다음 (　) 안에서 알맞은 말을 골라 바르게 짝지은 것을 고르시오.

> ·Josh (elected, was elected) leader by us.
> ·Someone (stole, stolen, was stolen) my car.

① was elected - stole
② was elected - stolen
③ was elected - was stolen
④ elected - stole
⑤ elected - was stolen

[13–15] 다음 보기에서 우리말에 알맞은 것을 골라 빈칸에 쓰시오.

> at　with　in　about　of

13 Bruce was worried ＿＿＿＿ his first test.
Bruce는 그의 첫 번째 시험에 대해 걱정했다.

14 I was surprised ＿＿＿＿ the beautiful house.
나는 아름다운 집에 놀랐다.

15 Jessica is pleased ＿＿＿＿ the present.
Jessica는 그 선물로 즐겁다.

16 다음 문맥상 빈칸에 알맞은 것을 고르시오.

> I have played the same video game since last month.
> So I am tired ＿＿＿＿ it.

① to
② with
③ of
④ by
⑤ in

17 다음 문장을 수동태로 바꾸었을 때 빈칸에 알맞은 말을 고르시오.

> I saw a dog cross the street.
> → A dog was seen _____ the street by me.

① cross
② crossed
③ crossing
④ to cross
⑤ for cross

[18-19] 다음을 수동태로 바꿀 때 빈칸에 알맞은 말을 써 넣으시오.

18

> Paul heard me play the piano.
> → I was heard _____ by Paul.

19

> Jane bought him a bag.
> → _____ was bought _____ by Jane.

20 주어진 문장을 수동태로 옳게 바꾼 것을 고르시오.

> We call her Gabby.

① She is called us by Gabby.
② Gabby is called her by us.
③ Gabby is called us by her.
④ She is called Gabby by us.
⑤ Gabby is called us by she.

[01–03] 다음 문장을 수동태로 바르게 옮긴 것을 고르시오.

01

> A boy bought some cookies.

① A boy is buying some cookies.
② Some cookies was bought by a boy.
③ Some cookies are bought by a boy.
④ Some cookies were bought by a boy.
⑤ Some cookies will be bought by a boy.

02

> My dog caught the ball.

① The ball is caught by my dog.
② The ball was caught by my dog.
③ The ball were caught by my dog.
④ My dog was catching the ball.
⑤ My dog catches the ball.

03

> I will read a book.

① I read a book by myself.
② A book is read by I.
③ A book is read by me.
④ A book will be read by I.
⑤ A book will be read by me.

04 다음 문장에서 틀린 부분을 찾아 바르게 고치시오.

> A beautiful music is being playing by an orchestra. 아름다운 음악이 오케스트라에 의해서 연주되어지고 있는 중이다.

_____ → _____

[05–06] 다음을 수동태로 바꿀 때, 빈칸에 들어갈 말로 알맞은 것을 고르시오.

05

> She must finish the homework.
> →The homework must _____ by her.

① finished
② being finished
③ be finish
④ be finished
⑤ been finished

06

> Sam Kim has made this pasta.
> →This pasta _____ by Sam Kim.

① is made
② was made
③ has being made
④ has be made
⑤ has been made

07 다음 주어진 문장을 능동태로 바르게 옮긴 것을 고르시오.

> A delicious chicken is being cooked by my mom.

① My mom cooks a delicious chicken.
② My mom is cooking a delicious chicken.
③ My mom cooked a delicious chicken.
④ My mom will cook a delicious chicken.
⑤ My mom be cooking a delicious chicken.

08 다음 빈칸에 들어갈 말이 바르게 짝지어진 것을 고르시오.

> He gave me a book.
> → I was _____ a book by ____.

① gave - he
② gave - him
③ given - he
④ given - him
⑤ given - his

09 다음 우리말에 맞게 빈칸에 들어갈 말을 고르시오.

> A teddy bear was made _____ me by him.
> 곰인형이 그에 의해서 나를 위하여 만들어졌다.

① to
② of
③ for
④ by
⑤ with

10 다음을 수동태로 만들 때, 빈칸에 알맞은 말을 쓰시오.

> He saw her go out.
> → She was seen _____ by him.

11 다음 빈칸에 공통으로 들어갈 전치사를 고르시오.

> · A question was asked ___ me by him.
> · The chair is made ___ plastic.

① by
② with
③ in
④ at
⑤ of

12 다음 중 어법상 <u>틀린</u> 문장을 고르시오.

① They were watched to fight by me.
② I was made to clean the dishes by my sister.
③ He was helped to order a drink by me.
④ She was had to buy pizza by her mom.
⑤ The thief was seen to sneak in by the police.

sneak in 몰래 들어가다

13 다음 빈칸에 with가 들어가지 <u>않는</u> 것을 고르시오.

① I am pleased ____ the food.
② The guests were satisfied ____ the event.
③ A theater was crowded ____ people.
④ The bottle was filled ____ cranberry juice.
⑤ She was interested ____ mathematics.

[14–15] 다음 대화를 읽고 물음에 답하시오.

Harry : Hello, Irene. How are you doing?
Irene : Not good.
Harry : What's wrong?
Irene : I have much stress. I am
  ⓐ_____ doing too many things.
Harry : I think you should take a break.
Irene : You're right. Thank you for your advice.
Harry : You're welcome.

14 이 상황을 표현하는 수동태 문장을 ( )안의 단어를 이용하여 영작하시오.

Irene은 휴식을 취할 것을 Harry로부터 조언 받았다.
→ *Irene* _____
  by *Harry*. (advise, take a break)

15 문맥에 맞게 ⓐ에 들어갈 말을 고르시오.

① satisfied with
② disappointed at
③ worried about
④ tired with
⑤ pleased with

16 다음 간접목적어를 주어로 하여 수동태 문장을 만든 것들 중 올바른 것을 고르시오.

① She was sent a letter by him.
② He was passed a ball by his friend.
③ I was read a book by my mom.
④ We were written letters by our cousins.
⑤ I was given a musical ticket by my friend.

17 다음 밑줄 친 부분이 어색한 것을 고르시오.

① The minister is worried about economy.
② He was tired of waiting for her.
③ She is involved in this matter.
④ I was disappointed at his being angry.
⑤ The book is covered from leather.

minister 장관   leather 가죽

18 다음 중 맞는 표현에 O표 하시오.

Mom called dad honey.
→ (Dad / Honey) was called (dad / honey) by (mom / dad).

[14-15] 다음 대화를 읽고 물음에 답하시오.

It was twelve o'clock at night. I was awake because I could not sleep. Suddenly, the door was ⓐ_____ ____ someone. I was so scared. Then, I realized that it was my brother.
He was ⓑ_____ ____ come home by me. (see) I told him not to be so late. He was sorry to scare me.

wake 깨어있는   suddenly 갑자기

19 ⓐ의 빈칸에 들어갈 올바른 말을 고르시오.

① open by
② open with
③ opened by
④ opened to
⑤ opened with

20 주어진 괄호 안의 단어를 이용해서 ⓑ의 빈칸을 바르게 채워 보시오.

ⓑ : _____ _____

Chapter 7

완료

현재 완료란?

'have+과거분사'의 형태로 '과거+현재'의 개념이며, 과거의 상태나 동작이 현재까지 연관되어 있는 것을 나타내는 동사의 시제를 말한다.

 계속

과거는 과거에 있었던 사실을 말한다.

ex. Uncle lived in America. 삼촌은 미국에 살았다. (현재는 어디에 살고 있는지 알 수 없음)

현재완료는 '과거 + 현재'의 의미로 과거부터 현재(지금)까지 계속되고 있는 것을 말한다.

ex. Uncle **has lived** in America since 2002. 삼촌은 2002년부터 미국에 살고 있다.
(현재도 미국에서 살고 있음.)

= Uncle started to live in America in 2002. + He still lives in America.
삼촌은 2002년에 미국에서 살기 시작했다.   그는 아직도 미국에서 살고 있다.

결과

과거는 과거에 있었던 사실을 말한다.

ex. Jane lost her ring. Jane은 그녀의 반지를 잃어버렸다. (현재(지금) 그 반지를 찾았는지 아닌지는 알 수 없음.)

현재완료는 '과거 + 현재'의 의미로 과거에 있었던 일이 현재도 그 상태 그대로인 것을 말한다.

ex. Jane **has lost** her ring. Jane은 그녀의 반지를 잃어버렸다. (현재(지금) 아직 그 반지를 찾지 못했음.)

= Jane lost her ring. + She doesn't have it now.
Jane은 그녀의 반지를 잃어버렸다.   그녀는 지금도 그것을 가지고 있지 않다.

완료

과거는 과거에 있었던 사실을 말한다.

ex. He finished homework. 그는 숙제를 끝마쳤다.

현재완료는 '과거 + 현재'의 의미로 과거에 시작해서 현재 끝냈다는 것을 말한다.

ex. He **has just finished** homework. 그는 이제 막 숙제를 끝마쳤다.

경험

과거는 과거에 있었던 사실을 말한다.

ex. She went to China. 그녀는 중국에 갔다. (그녀가 현재는 어디에 있는지 모름.)

현재완료는 '과거 + 현재'의 뜻으로, 과거에서 현재 까지 있었던 경험을 말한다.

ex. She **has been** to China twice. 그녀는 중국에 두 번 갔다 온 적이 있다. (현재는 돌아와 있다.)

UNIT 1

주의해야할 현재완료

1 have been to, have gone to, have been in

have been to	～에 가 본 적이 있다	경험
have gone to	～로 가 버렸다 (～로 가고 없다)	결과
have been in	～에 (계속) 있다 (～에서 지내고 있다)	계속

ex. Tom **has been to** Seoul. Tom은 서울에 가 본 적이 있다.

Tom **has gone to** Seoul. Tom은 서울로 가 버렸다.

Tom **has been in** Seoul. Tom은 서울에서 (계속) 있다.

> *Tip!* have been in 과 have been at
> have been in ~ : 대개 넓은 장소 (도시, 나라... 등)
> have been at ~ : 대개 좁은 장소 (사무실, 마을... 등)

* have (has) gone to는 주어로 1인칭(I, We)과 2인칭(You)을 쓸 수 없다.
문장의 의미로 볼 때 있을 수 없는 상황이 되기 때문이다.

ex. ~~I~~ have gone to Tokyo. 나는 도쿄로 가버렸다. (지금 나는 여기에 없다?)

~~We~~ have gone to Tokyo. 우리는 도쿄로 가버렸다. (지금 우리는 여기에 없다?)

~~You~~ have gone to Tokyo. 너는 도쿄로 가버렸다. (지금 너는 여기에 없다?)

다음 중 알맞은 것을 골라 보자.

1   He **has been in** Paris. 그는 파리에   (가 본적이 있다, 가버렸다, (계속 있다))

      He **has gone to** Paris. 그는 파리에   (가 본적이 있다, 가버렸다, 계속 있다)

      He **has been to** Paris. 그는 파리에   (가 본적이 있다, 가버렸다, 계속 있다)

2   They **have been to** Jim's house. 그들은 Jim의 집에   (가 본적이 있다, 가버렸다, 계속 있다)

      They **have been in** Jim's house. 그들은 Jim의 집에   (가 본적이 있다, 가버렸다, 계속 있다)

      They **have gone to** Jim's house. 그들은 Jim의 집에   (가 본적이 있다, 가버렸다, 계속 있다)

다음 중 알맞은 것을 골라 보자.

1   그녀는 이태리로 가버렸다.   She (has been to, (has gone to), has been in) Italy.

      그녀는 이태리에 가 본 적이 있다.   She (has been to, has gone to, has been in) Italy.

      그녀는 이태리에 계속 있다.   She (has been to, has gone to, has been in) Italy.

2   Jenny는 W호텔에 가 본적이 있다.   Jenny (has been to, has gone to, has been in) the W hotel.

      Jenny는 W호텔에 계속 있다.   Jenny (has been to, has gone to, has been in) the W hotel.

      Jenny는 W호텔로 가버렸다.   Jenny (has been to, has gone to, has been in) the W hotel.

다음 중 알맞은 것을 골라 보자.

1   I have (been to , gone to) the jazz festival before.

2   Have you ever (been to, gone to) China ?

3   Jack has (been to, gone to) L. A. (He is in L.A. now.)

4   He has never (been to, been in) Time Square.

5   We have (been to, been in) the office since 7 a.m.

6   Mom has (gone to, been to) Greece. (She is in Greece now.)

7   The fox has (been to, been in) the cave for a few days.

8   We have (been to, gone to) his office three times.

9   They have (gone to, been to) the cafe to meet Tom. (They are in the cafe now.)

10   Jinho has (been in, been to) Sydney to study. (He is in Sydney now.)

11   We have never (been to, gone to) Mr. Brown's.

12   Cathy has (been in, been to) her room for an hour.

13   I have (been to, been in) my friend's house since last Thursday.

14   He has (been to, gone to) his hometown. (He is in his hometown now.)

15   How long has he (been in, been to) the army?

---

festival 축제   Greece 그리스   Sydney 시드니   country 나라   army 군대   hometown 고향

우리말에 알맞게 문장을 완성해 보자.

1 He _has gone to_ the library to do his research. (He is not here now.)

그는 연구를 하기 위해 도서관에 가 버렸다. (그는 지금 이곳에 없다.)

2 I _____ the bathroom fixing my make up for 30 minutes.

나는 화장을 고치기 위하여 30분 동안 화장실에 있었다. (지금도 화장실에 있다)

3 She _____ France at least three times.

그녀는 적어도 3번 프랑스에 가 본적이 있다.

4 We _____ the classroom waiting for our teacher.

우리는 우리의 선생님을 기다리면서 교실에 있었다. (지금도 교실에 있다)

5 She _____ Harvard University to make a speech.

그녀는 연설하기 위해 하버드 대학에 가 본적이 있다.

6 Ann _____ bed already. (She is on the bed now.)

Ann은 이미 잠자러 가 버렸다. (그녀는 지금 침대에 있다.)

7 He _____ New York since he got his new job.

그는 새로운 직업을 구한 이후로 뉴욕에서 지내고 있다. (지금도 뉴욕에 있다)

8 They _____ Hawaii to learn how to surf. (They aren't here now.)

그들은 서핑하는 법을 배우기 위해 하와이로 가버렸다.

9 The president _____ many different states recently.

대통령은 최근에 많은 다른 주를 가 본 적이 있다.

10 We _____ the Olympic Park twice.

우리는 올림픽 공원을 두 번 가 본 적이 있다.

---

research 연구   make up 화장   at least 적어도   make a speech 연설하다   different 다른
recently 최근에

우리말에 알맞게 문장을 완성해 보자.

1 Our dog *has been to* the vet many times.

우리 개는 수의사에게 여러 번 간 적이 있다.

2 Mom   the pharmacy to pick up her medicine. (She is not here now.)

엄마는 약을 가지러 약국에 갔다.

3 The reporter   the scene. (He is still there.)

그 기자는 현장으로 갔다.

4 George   the recording studio since 10 a.m.

George는 오전 10시부터 녹음실에 있었다.

5 Helen   several cooking classes before.

Helen은 전에 여러 요리 강습에 가 본 적이 있다.

6 Somebody   my room. (He is still there.)

누군가 나의 방에 들어와 있다.

7 How many times   you   Russia?

너는 몇 번이나 러시아에 가 본 적이 있니?

8 How long   he   Seoul?

그는 얼마나 오랫동안 서울에서 지내고 있니?

9 The patients   the hospital since last month.

그 환자들은 지난 달부터 병원에 와 있다.

10 Grandmother   the nursing home. (she is not here now.)

할머니는 요양원으로 가셨다.

---

pharmacy 약국   **reporter** 기자   **scene** 현장   **several** 여러, 몇 몇   **recording studio** 녹음실
Russia 러시아   **nursing home** 요양원

UNIT 2

현재완료진행과 과거완료

1 현재완료진행

> have (has) been + ~ing : 과거에서 현재까지의 계속해서 진행되는 '동작'을 나타낸다.

ex. It **has been raining** for 5 days. 5일 동안 비가 오고 있는 중이다. (지금도 비가 오고 있음)

It started to rain 5 days ago. + It is raining now.

5일 전에 비가 오기 시작했다.   지금도 비가 오고 있는 중이다.

단, 상태를 나타내는 동사는 현재완료진행형을 사용하지 않는다.

~~I have been knowing~~ him for 7 years.

상태를 나타내는 동사 : know, love, have, like, exist, resemble.....

2 과거완료

> had + p.p

'과거의 이전'에서부터 있었던 일이 '과거'의 어느 시점까지 영향을 미치는 경우를 말하며 현재 완료와 똑같이
완료, 경험, 계속, 결과의 용법이 있다.

ex. I **had met** him twice, before he **left** Korea. (경험)
　　　 과거 완료　　　　　　　　　　　　　　　 과거

그가 한국을 떠나기 전에, 나는 그를 두 번 만난 적이 있었다.

두 개의 과거 중에서 더 과거(대과거)를 나타낼 때도 사용한다.

ex. She **found** the pen that she **had lost** yesterday. 그녀는 어제 잃어버렸던 펜을 찾았다.
　　　　 과거　　　　　　　　　　　　　 대과거

Tip! 단, 동시 발생일 때에는 둘 다 과거를 사용한다.
　　　 ex. As soon as she **saw** me, she **started** to cry. 그녀는 나를 보자마자, 울기 시작했다.
　　　　　　　　　　　 과거　　　　　　 과거

주어진 문장을 지시대로 바꿔 보자.

1 They have read comic books.

〈현재완료진행〉 They *have been reading* comic books.

〈과 거 완 료〉 They *had read* comic books.

2 He taught English.

〈현재완료진행〉 He English.

〈과 거 완 료〉 He English.

3 My sister watched musical.

〈과 거 완 료〉 My sister musical.

〈현재완료진행〉 My sister musical.

4 We have visited the orphanage.

〈과 거 완 료〉 We the orphanage.

〈현재완료진행〉 We the orphanage.

5 They worked very hard.

〈현재완료진행〉 They very hard.

〈과 거 완 료〉 They very hard.

comic book 만화책   musical 뮤지컬   orphanage 고아원

실력 TEST

다음 중 알맞은 것을 골라 보자.

1 그는 약 5시간째 무엇인가를 만들고 있는 중이다.

He (was making, has been making) something for about five hours.

2 나는 아까부터 나의 목걸이를 찾고 있는 중이다.

I (have looking, have been looking) for my necklace for some time.

3 그녀는 그녀의 일생동안 아무도 사랑하지 않았다.

She (has loved, has been loving) nobody in her life.

4 나의 남동생은 2시간 동안 나의 컴퓨터를 사용하고 있는 중이다.

My brother (has been using, had used) my computer for 2 hours.

5 나는 그녀를 10년 동안 알고 지내고 있다.

I (have known, have been known) her for 10 years.

6 그는 모든 그의 돈을 다 써버렸으므로, 그는 돈이 없었다.

As he (have spent, had spent) all his money, he (had, have had) no money.

7 Tom은 Jack이 그의 친구와 함께 가버렸다고 나에게 말했다.

Tom (told , had told) me that Jack (went, had gone) with his friend.

8 Mary는 신문을 읽었기 때문에, 그것을 알고 있었다.

Mary (knows, knew) it because she (read, had read) the newspaper.

9 그 개는 우리를 보자마자 짖기 시작했다.

As soon as the dog (saw, had seen) us, it (started, had started) to bark.

10 그녀는 빵을 구운 후, 그녀는 그것을 냄새 맡았다.

After she (baked, had baked) bread, she (smelled, had smelled) it.

[01–03] 우리말에 알맞은 것을 고르시오.

01

> 우리는 러시아에 가 본 적이 있다.
> We _____ Russia.

① have been to
② has been to
③ have been in
④ has been in
⑤ have gone to

02

> 그녀는 파리에서 계속 지내고 있다.
> She _____ Paris.

① have been to
② has been to
③ have been in
④ has been in
⑤ have gone to

03

> 그들은 미국으로 가버렸다.
> They _____ America.

① have been to
② has been to
③ have been in
④ has been in
⑤ have gone to

04 다음 중 틀린 곳을 찾아 바르게 고치시오.

> Uncle has gone to Vietnam.
> 삼촌은 베트남에 가본 적이 있다.

_____ → _____

05 ( ) 안의 동사를 사용하여 현재완료진행형으로 빈칸을 채워 보시오.

> 그는 약 한 시간 동안 샤워하고 있는 중이다. (take)
> He _____
> a shower for about 1 hour.

06 다음 중 어법상 옳은 것을 고르시오.

① Mary has be singing since 10 a.m.
② He have been fixing his cell-phone.
③ We have studying fine art.
④ Mom has been working for 3 hours.
⑤ They have been play soccer for 2 hours.

07 다음 두 문장의 빈칸에 공통으로 들어갈 말을 고르시오.

> Tommy has _____ planting a tree.
> They have _____ in Seoul since 2007.

① be
② being
③ been
④ go
⑤ gone

08 다음 빈칸에 알맞은 것을 고르시오.

> My brother went to the school, and he isn't at home now.
> → My brother _____ to the school.

① go
② goes
③ has been
④ have gone
⑤ has gone

09 다음 ( ) 안의 동사를 알맞은 형태로 바꾸시오.

> I met him at a camp when we were teenagers. Since that time, we (know) each other.

→ _____

10 다음 빈칸에 알맞은 것을 고르시오.

> It _____ for a week.
> 일주일 동안 눈이 오고 있는 중이다. (지금도 오고 있다.)

① has been snowed
② was snowing
③ had snowed
④ has been snowing
⑤ had been snowing

11 우리말 뜻과 같도록 ( ) 안의 단어를 바르게 배열하시오.

> Bill은 서울에 세 번 가 본 적이 있다.
> (has, three times, to, been, Seoul)

→ Bill _____

_____ .

12 다음 빈칸에 알맞은 것을 고르시오.

> He lost the pen that he _____ for his birthday gift the day before.

① got
② gotten
③ had gotten
④ gets
⑤ have gotten

13 다음 빈칸에 알맞은 말을 고르시오.

> Andy began to wait for a bus 30 minutes ago, and he is still waiting for a bus.
> = Andy ＿＿＿＿＿＿ for a bus for 30 minutes

① is been waiting
② has been waited
③ has been waiting
④ had being waited
⑤ had be waiting

14 다음 대화의 빈칸에 알맞은 것을 고르시오.

> *Lily* : ＿＿＿＿＿＿＿＿＿＿
> *Serena* : No, I haven't. Let's go to the park next time.

① Do you like to go to the park?
② Do you have gone to the park?
③ Did you go to the park?
④ Have you ever been to the park?
⑤ Do you go to the park?

15 다음 빈칸에 알맞은 것을 고르시오.

> Nancy ate out for lunch after she ＿＿＿＿＿＿ the project.

① completed
② had completed
③ will complete
④ complete
⑤ have completed

eat out 외식하다

16 빈칸에 들어갈 말로 알맞게 짝지어진 것을 고르면?

> Tom은 어제 샀던 지우개를 그녀에게 줬다.
> Tom ＿＿＿＿ her the eraser that he ＿＿＿＿ yesterday.

① had given-bought
② has given-bought
③ has given-has bought
④ gave-has bought
⑤ gave-had bought

[17–18] 다음 대화를 읽고 물음에 답하시오.

Penny : Hey, Tom. How was your vacation?

Tom : Hi, Penny. It was great!
_____ ⓐ _____ ?

Penny : No, I haven't. Have you?

Tom : Yes. I went back home last week. I stayed in Rome. It is a very beautiful city.

Penny : I really want to visit there. By the way, Did you hear about Mary?

Tom : No. When will she be back?

Penny : She ___ ⓑ ___ to Canada. She may not be back. It's so sad. I didn't say goodbye to her.

17 다음 우리말과 뜻이 같도록 밑줄 친 ⓐ에 알맞은 말을 쓰시오.

너는 로마에 가 본 적 있니?
= _____ Rome?

18 밑줄 친 ⓑ에 알맞은 것을 고르시오.

① goes
② went
③ have been
④ have gone
⑤ has gone

[19–20] 다음 중 **틀린** 문장을 고르시오.

19 ① They have been playing soccer for 3 hours.
② Tom has been eating pizza for 1 hour.
③ Uncle has been sleeping on the sofa for 5 hours.
④ I have been knowing Jane for 5 years.
⑤ It has been snowing for 3 days.

20 ① After Tom had finished homework, he turned on TV.
② Before Kate went to bed, she had brushed her teeth.
③ I had seen the video twice, before Jimmy saw it yesterday.
④ Susan found out the ring that she had lost a week ago.
⑤ He called Liz once before she had moved to LA.

[01–03] 다음 빈칸에 알맞은 것을 고르시오.

01

> Sue는 베이징에 가 본 적이 있다.
> Sue _____ Beijing.

① went to
② was going to
③ has been to
④ has gone to
⑤ has been in

02

> Amy는 로마로 가 버렸다. (로마로 가고 없다)
> Amy _____ Rome.

① went to
② was going to
③ has been to
④ has gone to
⑤ has been in

03

> Sam은 도쿄에서 (계속) 지내고 있다.
> Sam _____ Tokyo.

① stayed in
② was going to
③ has been to
④ has gone to
⑤ has been in

04 다음 두 문장의 빈 칸에 공통으로 들어갈 말을 고르시오.

> • Cindy has _____ shopping for an hour.
> • Our family has _____ in New York for 2 years.

① be
② been
③ being
④ gone
⑤ go

05 다음 문장의 괄호 안에서 알맞은 것에 O표 해보세요.

> • I have been (at / in) a small village.
> • They have been (at / in) Mongolia.

Mongolia 몽고

06 다음 중 어색한 문장을 고르시오.

① I have gone to Paris.
② She has gone to London.
③ He has been at the dormitory.
④ They have been in Africa.
⑤ Uncle has been to Argentina.

dormitory 기숙사

07 다음 괄호 안의 단어가 들어갈 알맞은 자리를 고르시오.

> (since)
> ① I ② have been ③ waiting ④ for her call ⑤ yesterday.

08 다음 각 빈칸에 들어갈 말이 알맞게 짝지어진 것을 고르시오.

> I _____ movie with him twice, before he _____ Seoul.
> 그가 서울을 떠나기 전에, 나는 그와 영화를 두 번 본적이 있었다.

① watched - left
② watched - had left
③ had watched - leaves
④ had watched - left
⑤ had watched - had left

09 다음 문장을 바르게 해석한 것을 고르시오.

> He has been playing computer games since twelve o' clock.

① 그는 12시에 컴퓨터 게임을 했다.
② 그는 과거에 12시에 컴퓨터 게임을 한 적이 있다.
③ 그는 12시부터 컴퓨터 게임을 하다 지금은 그만두었다.
④ 그는 12시간 동안 컴퓨터 게임을 하는 중이다.
⑤ 그는 12시부터 지금까지 컴퓨터 게임을 하고 있는 중이다.

10 다음 중 옳은 문장을 고르시오.

① They have been exercising for 2hours.
② I have been belonging to this country.
③ The TV have been existing since 1970s.
④ She has been having two brothers.
⑤ He has been remembering my name.

belong to ～에 속하다   exist 존재하다

11 다음 문장을 바르게 영작한 것을 모두 고르시오.

> 일주일 동안 비가 오고 있는 중이다. (지금도 비가 오고 있음)

① It rained for a week.
② It was raining for a week.
③ It is been rained for a week.
④ It has been raining for a week.
⑤ It had been raining for a week.

12 다음 두 문장의 뜻이 같도록 빈칸을 바르게 채워 보시오. (현재완료진행형 사용)

> A baby started to sleep 5 hours ago. + The baby is still sleeping.
> = A baby _____
>   for 5 hours.

13 다음 문장의 밑줄 친 부분을 바르게 고쳐보시오.

> We <u>have been knowing</u> each other for 10 years.
> 우리는 10년 동안 서로 알고 지내고 있다.

have been knowing → _____

[14–15] 다음 글을 읽고 물음에 답하시오.

> Noel, my friend, is from England. He ⓐ <u>has gone to</u> many countries because he travels a lot. It is his first time visiting Korea. His parents were worried. Because Noel ⓑ _____(break) his arm before he left home.

14 ⓐ의 어법상 어색한 부분을 바르게 고치시오.

ⓐ has gone to → _____

15 다음 ( )안의 주어진 단어를 바르게 고쳐 ⓑ의 빈칸을 채워보시오.

ⓑ : _____

16 다음 중 어법상 옳은 것을 고르시오.

① I have be walking since morning.
② We have studying literature.
③ They have been playing soccer for 2 hours.
④ She has being cooking a cake.
⑤ You have been worked for all day.

17 우리말 뜻과 같도록 괄호 안의 단어를 바르게 배열하시오.

> 대통령은 북한에 두 번 방문한 적이 있다.
> President (has, twice, to, been, North Korea).

President _____.

18 괄호 안의 동사를 사용하여 우리말에 알맞게 빈 칸을 채워 보시오. (현재완료 진행형)

> 그는 약 두 시간 동안 저녁을 먹고 있는 중이다.
> (아직도 먹고 있다.)
> He _____
> dinner for about two hours. (eat)

19 다음 빈칸에 알맞은 것을 고르시오.

> She got a dog that she _____ for her birthday gift.

① was wanted
② has been wanting
③ had wanted
④ will want
⑤ has wanted

20 다음 빈칸에 알맞은 것을 고르시오.

> *Dan :* _____
> *Sarah :* No, I haven't. Let's go now.

① Do you like to go to the restaurant?
② Do you have gone to the restaurant?
③ Did you go to the restaurant?
④ Have you been to the restaurant?
⑤ Do you go to the restaurant?

종합문제

01 다음 빈칸에 알맞은 전치사를 고르시오.

> It was hard _____ him to work at night.
> 밤에 일하는 것은 그에게 힘들었다.

① in
② at
③ by
④ for
⑤ of

02 다음 빈칸에 알맞은 것을 고르시오.

> Tom remembers _____ the vase then.
> Tom은 그때 꽃병을 깨뜨린 것을 기억하고 있다.

① break
② broke
③ broken
④ to break
⑤ breaking

03 우리말과 같은 뜻이 되도록 빈칸에 알맞은 말을 쓰시오.

> 네가 나를 치료해주다니 정말 착하구나.
> → It is very good _____ _____ to cure me.

cure 치료하다

04 다음 문장과 의미가 같은 것을 고르시오.

> The boy is too young to go there.

① The boy is so young because he can't go there.
② The boy is so young that he can go there.
③ The boy is so young that he can't go there.
④ The boy is not young, so he can go there.
⑤ The boy is so young, but he can go there.

05 다음 밑줄 친 부분 중 틀린 것을 바르게 고쳐 쓰시오.

It is <u>nice</u> <u>for</u> <u>him</u> <u>to help</u> <u>them</u>.
그들을 도와주다니 그는 친절하구나.

_____ → _____

nice 멋진, 친절한

06 두 문장의 뜻이 같도록 빈칸에 알맞은 말을 쓰시오.

Joseph swims well.
= Joseph is good at _____

07 다음 빈칸에 알맞은 것을 고르시오.

Don't forget _____ the window
when you leave home.
네가 집을 나설 때 창문 닫는 것을 잊지 마라.

① close
② closed
③ to close
④ closing
⑤ to closing

[08–09] 다음을 분사구문으로 바르게 바꾼 것을 고르시오.

08

As I have no money, I can't buy
the ring.
= _____ , I can't buy the ring.

① Had no money
② To have no money
③ Having no money
④ I having no money
⑤ To having no money

09

While she was walking along the
river, she saw an old friend.
= _____ along the river, she
saw an old friend.

① Being walking
② Walking
③ having walking
④ To walking
⑤ For walking

10 다음 중 **틀린** 곳을 바르게 고쳐 쓰시오.

> Susan is looking forward to have her birthday party.

_____ → _____

12 밑줄 친 말 대신에 쓸 수 있는 것을 고르시오.

> <u>Having no food</u>, I couldn't give you anything.

① If I have no food
② When I have no food
③ Though I had no food
④ As I had no food
⑤ Because I have no food

11 다음을 분사구문으로 바꿀 때 빈칸에 알맞은 말을 써 넣으시오.

> Because she was too sick, she didn't go to the church.
> = _____,
> she didn't go to church.

[13–14] 다음 문장을 과거형으로 바꿀 때, 빈칸에 알맞은 말을 쓰시오.

13
> I must give the doll to her.
> → I _____ give the doll to her.

14
> Tom can ride a skateboard.
> → Tom _____ ride a skateboard.

[15–16] 다음 문장을 미래형으로 바꿀 때, 빈칸에 알맞은 말을 쓰시오.

15

Susan must finish the work today.
→ Susan _____
the work today.

16

She can cook the fish.
→ She _____
the fish.

17 다음 빈칸에 우리말과 알맞은 것을 고르시오.

그는 그의 남동생을 위해 닭죽을 만드는데 익숙해졌다.
He _____ the chicken soup
for his brother.

① used to making
② got used to make
③ is used to make
④ is used making
⑤ got used to making

[18–19] 다음을 수동태로 바꿀 때 빈칸에 알맞은 말을 고르시오.

18

Koreans have built the ship.
= The ship _____ _____ _____
by Koreans.

① have be built
② has be built
③ have been built
④ has been built
⑤ has being built

19

Dad is driving a taxi.
= A taxi _____ _____ _____
by dad.

① is be driven
② is being driven
③ is being driving
④ is be driving
⑤ is been driving

20 분사구문으로 바꾸어 쓴 문장에서 **틀린** 곳을 고르시오.

> As Billy was honest, he was loved by people.
> = ① Being ② honest, ③ he ④ was loved ⑤ by people.

21 다음을 ( ) 안의 지시대로 바꾸어 쓸 때, 차례대로 알맞은 것을 고르시오.

> She plays the cello.
> → She _____ the cello. (현재완료진행형)
> → She _____ the cello. (과거완료)

① has be playing - had played
② has being played - had played
③ has be playing - had been played
④ has being played - had be played
⑤ has been playing - had played

[22~23] 다음 대화를 읽고 물음에 답하시오.

> *Jenny* : What do you want to eat for lunch?
> *Lucy* : Umm... actually I am not hungry. ⓐ I am so full that I can't eat now. I just need something cold ___ⓑ___ drink. Are you hungry?
> *Jenny* : Yeah... I'll get something ___ⓒ___ eat...like sandwich...or bread. And I'll buy juice for you.

22 다음 밑줄 친 ⓐ와 의미가 같도록 빈칸을 채우시오.

> I am so full that I can't eat now.
> = I am _____ _____ _____ eat now.

23 다음 밑줄 친 ⓑ와 ⓒ에 공통으로 들어갈 말을 고르시오.

① to
② in
③ for
④ of
⑤ on

[24–25] 다음 글을 읽고 물음에 답하시오.

Long ago, there was a wonderful woman in this town. Her beauty was well-known ___ⓐ___ people. A lot of men wanted to marry her. But only one man was chosen by her. The man was very brave and smart. ⓑ The man built a big house for her. They moved to the new house and lived happily for a long time.

24 밑줄 친 ⓐ에 들어갈 알맞은 전치사를 고르시오.

① on
② to
③ for
④ in
⑤ with

25 밑줄 친 ⓑ를 수동태로 바꿀 때 알맞은 단어로 빈칸을 채우시오.

The man built a big house for her.
→ A big house _____ _____
   for her by the man.

01 다음 상황으로 보아 빈칸에 알맞은 말을 고르시오.

> I wanted to call Betty.
> So, I stopped _____ for a while.

① walk
② walked
③ walking
④ to walk
⑤ for walking

for a while 잠시 동안

02 다음 빈칸에 알맞은 말로 바르게 짝지어진 것을 고르시오.

> Sam is fond of _____ a story book.
> Julie is proud of _____ a good grade in her test.

① read - get
② to read - to get
③ to read - getting
④ reading - to get
⑤ reading - getting

03 다음 빈칸에 차례대로 알맞은 전치사를 고르시오.

> It is impossible _____ her to cross the river alone.
> It is very wise _____ you to quit smoking.

① to-to
② for-for
③ of-of
④ for-of
⑤ of-for

quit 끊다, 그만두다

04 다음 빈칸에 알맞지 <u>않은</u> 것을 고르시오.

> It was _____ of him to say that.

① wise
② kind
③ careless
④ stupid
⑤ difficult

05 다음 빈칸에 알맞은 것을 고르시오.

> I was busy _____ the cello.
>
> 나는 첼로를 연주하느라고 바빴다.

① play
② to play
③ playing
④ to playing
⑤ being played

06 우리말과 같은 뜻이 되도록 ( ) 안의 단어를 이용하여 빈칸에 알맞은 말을 쓰시오.

> 선생님에게 너의 보고서를 제출하는 것을 잊지 마라.
> → Don't forget _____ your
>   paper to the teacher. (turn in)

turn in 제출하다

07 다음 대화의 빈칸에 공통으로 들어갈 말로 알맞은 것을 고르시오.

> *Andy* : Could you stop _____ ?
>   노크 좀 그만 할래?
> *Sally* : Sorry but I cannot help
>   _____ .
>   미안하지만 노크를 하지 않을 수 없어.

① knock
② knocking
③ knocked
④ to knock
⑤ for knocking

08 다음을 같은 뜻이 되도록 할 때 빈칸에 알맞은 것을 고르시오.

> I don't know what to answer the
> question.
> = I don't know what _____
>   _____ _____ the question.

① I could answer
② I should answer
③ I might answer
④ I am to answer
⑤ I am answering

[09-10] 다음 ( ) 안의 단어를 우리말에 맞게 배열해 보시오.

09

그녀는 내일 할 중요한 어떤 일이 있다.
(she, tomorrow, to do, important, something, has)

→ _____
_____

10

그는 내일 할 많은 일이 있다.
(he, tomorrow, to do, a lot of, things, has)

→ _____
_____

[11-12] 다음을 같은 뜻의 문장으로 바꾸었을 때 빈칸에 알맞은 말을 쓰시오.

11

He is too old to live alone.
= He is so old _____ _____ _____
live alone.

12

She is smart enough to solve the riddle.
= She is so smart _____ _____
_____ solve the riddle.

13 다음 밑줄 친 부분을 분사구문으로 바르게 바꾼 것을 고르시오.

> <u>After I eat lunch</u>, I'll go out.

① Having eaten lunch
② Eaten lunch
③ Eating lunch
④ I eating lunch
⑤ Ate lunch

14 다음 문장을 분사구문으로 바르게 바꾼 것을 모두 고르시오.

> As Jane was too tired yesterday, she went to bed early.
> _____ , Jane went to bed early.

① Being too tired yesterday
② Having too tired yesterday
③ Too tiring yesterday
④ Too tired yesterday
⑤ To being too tired yesterday

[15–16] 다음을 분사구문을 바꾸었을 때, 빈칸에 들어갈 말로 알맞게 짝지어진 것을 고르시오.

15

> As Jimmy started early, he could arrive there in time.
> = _____ early, _____ could arrive there in time.

① Start - he
② Starting - he
③ Starting - Jimmy
④ Started - he
⑤ Started - Jimmy

16

> Because I was doing the dishes, I couldn't hear him come.
> = _____ the dishes, I couldn't hear him come.

① Doing
② Being doing
③ Been doing
④ Have been doing
⑤ Has been doing

17 다음 우리말과 일치하도록 빈칸에 알맞은 말을 고르시오.

> 그들이 웃는 것은 당연하다.
> They _____ laugh.

① may well
② had better
③ may as well
④ used to
⑤ would rather

[18–19] 다음 우리말과 일치하도록 빈칸에 알맞은 말을 써 넣으시오.

18

> 뒷마당에 우물이 있었다. (지금은 없다)
> There _____ a well in the backyard.

19

> 우리는 여기 사느니 차라리 런던으로 이사하는 편이 낫겠다.
> We would rather move to London _____ live here.

20 다음문장을 ( ) 안의 지시대로 바꿔 쓰시오.

> a) It rains a lot.
>   → It _____ a lot.
>   (현재완료진행형)
> b) Mom made some soup for us.
>   (과거완료)
>   → Mom _____ some soup for us.

21 다음 우리말과 같은 뜻이 되록 빈칸에 써 넣으시오.

> 나는 Sam이 그 영화를 보았다고 생각했다.
> I thought that Sam _____ the movie. (watch)

[22–23] 다음 글을 읽고 물음에 답하시오.

I remember ⓐ (go) to America last year. I went there to meet my cousin. She is studying to be a doctor. We visited her university. There were few students because it was during the vacation. But the university was great. Their basketball team was great, too. We took a picture together. She bought a university T-shirt to give to me. We spent a lot of time ___ⓑ___ together.

[24–25] 다음 글을 읽고 물음에 답하시오.

John and Thomas were playing in the playground. They played with a ball. ⓐ <u>They broke a window.</u> It was a mistake. They were scared because that window was Ron's. Ron was not a nice man. Anyway, John and Thomas went to Ron's house to apologize. They told him about the accident. Ron was surprised ___ⓑ___ the accident but Ron forgave them. It was lucky for John and Thomas.

22 밑줄 친 ⓐ에 (   ) 안의 동사를 알맞게 변형시켜 쓰시오.

→ _____

24 밑줄 친 ⓐ를 수동태로 바꿀 때 알맞은 말로 빈칸을 채우시오.

A window _____ them.

23 밑줄 친 ⓑ에 알맞은 것을 고르시오.

① talk
② to talk
③ talking
④ talked
⑤ to talking

25 밑줄 친 ⓑ에 들어갈 알맞은 전치사를 고르시오.

① at
② with
③ of
④ to
⑤ for

MEMO

GRAMMAR JOY
중등영문법
2a

정답 및 해설

Grammar Joy
중등 영문법

2a

정답과 해설

POLY BOOKS

Chapter 1
부정사 A

Unit 1
기초 TEST   p.14~15

Ⓐ **1** 그가 그 책을 읽는 것은, 그 책을 읽는 것은 **2** 아이들이 텐트에서 자는 것은, 텐트에서 자는 것은 **3** '아니오'라고 말하는 것은, 내가 '아니오'라고 말하는 것은

1 them **2** her ▶for+목적격 **3** us **4** you ▶of+목적격
5 Jane ▶Jane이 제 시간에 약을 복용하는 것은 중요합니다.

Ⓑ
1 good, nice, safe, necessary, easy, possible, important, difficult, dangerous, hard,
2 kind, careless, polite, foolish, wise, careful, rude, stupid, smart, brave, clever

기본 TEST   p.16~21

Ⓐ **1** for **2** of **3** of **4** of **5** for **6** for **7** of **8** of **9** for **10** of **11** for **12** for **13** of **14** for **15** for

Ⓑ **1** of **2** for **3** of **4** for **5** for **6** for **7** for **8** of **9** of **10** for **11** for **12** of **13** for **14** of **15** for

Ⓒ **1** for me **2** of him **3** of her **4** for you **5** of Jim **6** for us **7** of the girl **8** for them **9** for Amy **10** for him

Ⓓ **1** for you **2** for them **3** of James ▶James가 약자를 괴롭히는 사람에게 맞선 것은 용감했습니다. **4** for me **5** for her **6** for us **7** for you **8** for him **9** of her **10** for children ▶아이들이 낯선 사람을 따라가는 것은 위험합니다.

Ⓔ
1 그 경찰관이 / Jenny를 찾는 것은. for the police officer, to find out
2 원숭이들이 / 나무에 오르는 것은. It is easy, to climb up
3 그가 / 호랑이를 포획하는 것은. of him, to capture
4 그들이 / 아픈 사람들을 돌보는 것은.It is good, of them
5 Tom이 / 식사 전에 손을 씻는 것은. It is polite, to wash his hands
6 Mary가 / 그 남자를 신뢰하는 것은. It was foolish, of Mary
7 요리사가 / 모든 조리법을 외우는 것은. for a cook, to memorize
8 우리가 / 연예인들을 만나는 것은. for us, to see
9 네가 / 에스컬레이터에서 넘어지는 것은. It is careless, of you
10 그녀는 / 지금 표를 사는 것이. for her, to buy

Ⓕ **1** Tom이 / 너와 함께 있어주는 것은. of Tom, to be
2 그들이 / 금메달을 따는 것은. It is surprising, for them
3 내가 / 매운 고추를 먹는 것은. It is impossible, to eat
4 나의 상사가 / 회의를 연기하는 것은. for my boss, to put off
5 B메이 / 드럼을 연주하는 것은. It is nice(wonderful), to play ▶악기 앞에는 정관사 the가 붙습니다.
6 나의 아들이 / 매일 패스트푸드를 먹는 것은.It is terrible, for my son
7 그녀가 / Jane과 빈둥거리는 것은. It is foolish(stupid), of her
8 그 소방관이 / 불속에서 그 아기를 구조한 것은. of the fire-fighter, to rescue
9 학생들이 / 학교에 제 시간에 도착하는 것은. for students, to get
10 네가 / 칼을 안전하게 사용하는 것은. It is wise, to use

A

1 what she should do
▶의문사+to부정사 = 의문사+주어+should
2 where he should live
3 what she should say
4 when they should leave
5 how he should save

1 how to get there   **2** when to go
3 what to sell   **4** where to go on
5 when to call

B **1** what to learn, what I should learn
2 how to cook, how she should cook
3 when to call at, when I should call at
4 where to feed, where they should feed
5 what to buy, what he should buy
6 how to ride, how he should ride ▶방법은 how

Unit 2

A

1 anything sweet x / anything x to eat / anything sweet to eat
2 something special x / something special to buy / something x to buy
3 everything important to learn / everything x to learn / everything important x
4 nothing new x / nothing new to know / nothing x to know

A

1 something difficult to learn
▶something+형용사+to부정사
2 something unique to bring
3 anything to happen ▶anything+to부정사

4 something to wear
5 nothing special to say
6 something to clear up
7 anything unusual ▶~thing+형용사
8 something light to eat

B **1** 먹을 / 따뜻한 / (어떤)것. something warm to eat
2 딱딱한 / (어떤)것. anything hard
3 달콤한 / (어떤)것. something sweet
4 볼 / 재미있는 / (어떤)것. anything fun to watch
5 필요한 / 모든 것. everything necessary
6 읽을 / 흥미로운 / (어떤)것. something interesting to read
7 이해하기 / 어려운 / 아무 것. nothing hard to understand
8 줄 / 멋진 / (어떤)것. something nice to give
▶choose-chose-chosen
9 드문 / (어떤)일. something rare ▶어떤 드문 것
10 중요한 / (어떤)것. anything important

Unit 3

A

1 배우기에 충분히 재미있다. for me / 내가 배우기에 충분히 재미있다.
2 너무 위험해서 수영할 수 없다. for children / 너무 위험에서 어린이들이 수영할 수 없다.
3 이해하기에 충분히 쉽다. for me / 내가 이해하기에 충분히 쉽다
4 건너가기에 충분히 튼튼하다. for trucks / 트럭들이 건너가기에(건너갈 만큼) 충분히 튼튼하다
5 너무 좁아서 통과할 수 없다. for the bus / 너무 좁아서 그 버스가 통과할 수 없다

B **1** he, couldn't, 과거 **2** he, can't, 현재 ▶그는 너무 못생겨서 여자들의 시선을 받을 수가 없다. **3** they, couldn't, 과거 **4** she, could, 과거 ▶과거는 could를 사용합니다. **5** we, can, 현재 ▶you and I는 we로 받습니다.

1 I, couldn't, 과거 **2** Jim, can, 현재 **3** children, couldn't, 과거 **4** he, can, 현재 **5** she, couldn't, 과거

A

1 so, that, couldn't 　　2 that, she, could
3 so, that, he, can ▶bold=brave
4 so, sick, she, couldn't 　　5 lucky, that, could
6 so, it, can 　　7 that, he, can't
8 sick, he, couldn't 　　9 she, could
10 so, that, couldn't

B

1 so good that he can be
2 so rich that she can travel
3 so hungry that he couldn't walk
4 so late that I couldn't attend
▶나는 너무 늦게 출발해서 회의에 제 시간에 갈 수 없었습니다.
5 so strong that he can work

1 for him / so sweet that he couldn't eat
2 for me / so tall that I can't climb
3 for her / so much that she can buy
4 for Billy / so expensive that Billy couldn't
purchase ▶purchase=buy
5 the song / so popular that it can be
▶문장의 주어가 부정사의 의미상의 주어와 같습니다.

C

1 well enough to win
2 too busy to meet
3 patient enough to listen
4 too short to push
5 lucky enough to have
▶나는 좋은 선생님을 만날 만큼 운이 좋다.

1 big enough for us to get
2 too fast for him to stand
3 too complex for me to solve
4 big enough for her to put
5 too small for Jane to find

D

1 too excited to sit, so excited that we couldn't sit
▶too~to = so~ that 주어 can't/couldn't
2 tall enough to change, so tall that I can change
3 too busy to pick up, so busy that she couldn't
pick up

4 too badly to wait, so badly that he can't wait
▶bad 나쁜 badly 심하게
5 old enough to retire, so old that he can retire
6 brave enough to try, so brave that he could try
▶brave=bold=courageous

실력 TEST

p.36

A

1 나의 아들이, dry enough for my son to wear, so dry
that my son can wear them
2 그녀가, too small for her to put on, so small that
she couldn't put it on
3 그 소년들이, too deep for the boys to play in, so
deep that the boys can't play in it
4 내가, too bitter for me to take, so bitter that I
couldn't take it
5 농부들이, ripe enough for the farmers to pick, so
ripe that the farmers can pick them
6 아기들이, big enough for babies to play with, so
big that babies can play with them

내신대비1

p.37~40

01 ④　02 ②　03 ③　04 ④　05 how he
should ride　06 ③　07 ②　08 ③　09 ④
10 ④　11 ③　12 to wear warm → warm to
wear　13 good anything → anything good
14 ①　15 ④　16 that → to　17 ④　18 ②
19 so, I can't　20 ⑤

01 의미상의 주어가 다를 때는 for(of)+목적격을 사용합니다.
02 사람을 칭찬/비난할 때는 of를 사용합니.
03 칭찬/비난의 의미가 아닌 형용사는 for를 사용합니다.
04 의문사+to부정사 = 의문사+주어+should, where to go = where
she should go
05 의문사+to부정사 = 의문사+주어+should, how to ride = how he
should ride
06 something+형용사+to부정사
07 too ~to = so that 주어 can't

08 ~enough to = so~that 주어 can

09 ~enough to = so~that 주어 can

10 ⓑ enough old → old enough ⓑ weak too → too weak

11 for me: 의미상의 주어

12 nothing+형용사+to부정사

13 anything+형용사+to부정사

14 ① 이 가방은 그녀가 들 수 있을 만큼 작다. / 이 가방은 너무 작아 서 그녀가 들 수 없다.

15 ④ something to drink cold → something cold to drink

16 Kate는 너무 가난해서 핸드폰 요금을 낼 수 없었다.

17 so~that 주어 can't, 시제가 과거이므로 couldn't가 와야 합니다.

18 시제가 과거이므로 could가 와야 합니다.

19 too 형용사 for 의미상의 주어+to 동사 = so 형용사 that 의미상의 주어+동사

20 If it is too hard to handle, 만약 그것이 다루기에 너무 어렵다면

내신대비2
p.41~44

01 ① 02 ④ 03 ④ 04 ③ 05 cannot
06 ⑤ 07 ③ 08 ② 09 ⑤ 10 ② 11 ④
12 someone to lean on 13 everything useful to know 14 ⓐtoo heavy ⓑcould not 15 ③
16 ① 17 ⑤ 18 something nice to wear
19 a lot of things 20 she should

01 형용사(또는 부사)+enough to ~ 의 어순입니다.

02 주절의 동사가 과거(was)이므로 could를 사용합니다.

03 부정사의 의미상의 주어는 'for +목적격'이 to ~앞에 옵니다.

05 too ~ to …는 그 자체가 부정의 의미이므로 'so ~ that 주어 cannot …'으로 바꾸어 씁니다.

06 sorry 는 사람의 성격을 나타내는 형용사가 아니므로 of 대신 for를 사용합니다.

08 가주어는 it을 사용하며, stupid 는 사람의 성격을 나타내므로 of 를 사용합니다.

10 의문사 + to 부정사 = 의문사 + 주어 + should …

11 ~thing + 형용사 + to 부정사

15 of + 목적격 +to 부정사

16 ① can't → can

19 things 는 ~thing 이 아니라 보통명사이므로 'a lot of + things + to ~'의 어순을 가집니다.

20 문장의 주어(My sister)를 대명사(주격)로 받으므로 she should ~ 가 됩니다.

Chapter 2

부정사 B

Unit 1

기초 TEST
p.48~51

Ⓐ 1 him, Jimmy / 그를 Jimmy라고

2 Spider-Man, a hero / 스파이더맨을 영웅이라고

3 me, sad / 나를 슬프게

4 their children, smart / 그들의 아이들이 똑똑하다고

5 the door, open / 그 문을 열어둔 채로

1 to go to college, 대학에 가기를 / me, to go to college, 내가, 대학에 가기를

2 her, to leave Paris, 그녀가, 파리를 떠나기를 / to leave Paris, 파리를 떠나기를

3 to play outside 밖에서 놀기를 / her son, to play outside 그녀의 아들이, 밖에서 놀기를

Ⓑ 1 Tom을, 대장으로, elected, Tom, captain

2 나의 아기를, Paul이라고, named, my baby, Paul

3 그녀의 몸을, 날씬하게, kept, her body, slim

4 그가, 살아 있는 것을, found, him, alive

5 그녀의 남편을, honey라고, calls, her husband, "honey"

6 그녀를, 그의 아내로, made, her, his wife

7 나를, 작고 약하다고 considers, me, small and weak

8 그녀의 집이, 멋지다는 것을, found, her house, wonderful

9 그가, 친절하고 너그럽다고, think, him, kind and generous

10 그의 셔츠를, 더럽게, got, his shirt, dirty

Ⓒ 1 우리가, 더 오래 머물기를, want us to stay

2 그녀에게, 진정하라고, told her to calm down

3 그녀의 아들에게, 따뜻한 코트를 입으라고, advised her son to wear

4 나에게, 한 시간을 기다리라고, asked me to wait

5 그녀를, 우리의 모범으로, made her our role model

6 나에게, 파를 살 것을, reminded me to buy

7 그들이, '예'라고 대답하기를, expected them to say

8 그들에게, 전진하라고, ordered them to go

9 나에게, 게임을 멀리하라고, warned me to stay away from

10 아빠가, 은퇴하시길, doesn't want dad to retire

 D

1 그를, 우리 반의 반장으로, him, president of our class

2 나를, 홀로, me, alone

3 그의 엄마가, 건강하게 유지하기를, his mom, to keep

4 그것에게, "Moomoo"라고, it, "Moomoo"

5 그를, 개그맨으로, him, a comedian

6 Bill이, 매우 게으르다는 것을, Bill, very lazy

7 그 강아지를, 혼자, the puppy, alone

8 그 시계를, 'Big Ben'이라, the clock, "Big Ben"

9 그가, 진실을 말할 것을, him, to tell

10 그녀를, 편안하게, her, comfortable

기본 TEST   p.52~53

(A) 1 그에게, 휴식을 취하라고, advised, him, to take

2 내가, 그 학원에 갈 것을 asked, me, to go

3 그녀의 남편이, 낡은 정장을 입기를, want, her husband, to wear

4 Tom에게, 탁자의 다리를 고칠 것을, reminded, Tom, to fix

5 그녀에게, 문을 닫으라고, told, her, to shut

6 우리에게, 제시간에 오라고, warned, us, to be

7 그의 딸이, 그 대회에서 이기기를, wanted, his daughter, to win

8 조수에게, 그를 따라오라고, ordered, the assistant, to follow

9 나에게, 나의 남자친구와 헤어지라고, advised, me, to break up with

10 John에게, 그 사자를 죽이라고, ordered, John, to kill

 (B) 1 ○ 2 ✕ ▶hope는 목적보어가 있는 5형식문장을 만들 수 없습니다. 3 ○ 4 ○ 5 ✕ ▶decide는 목적보어가 있는 5형식 문장을 만들 수 없습니다. 6 ✕ 7 ○ 8 ○ 9 ✕ 10 ○ 11 ✕ 12 ○ 13 ✕ 14 ○ 15 ✕

Unit 2

기초 TEST   p.55~57

 (A)

1 그녀의 아들에게 집을 청소하게 시켰다. 그녀의 친구와 저녁을 먹었다.

2 우리에게 300개의 새 단어를 암기하게 시켰다(만들었다). 성적표를 만드셨다

3 많은 정보를 구했다. 그녀의 아들이 그의 친구들을 데려오게 시켰다(했다)

4 내가 거기에 가도록 허락했다. 그것을 합시다

5 그 노인이 그 짐꾸러미를 나르는 것을 도와주었다. 그 노인을 도왔다.

(B)

1 order, want, tell, ask, remind, advise, expect, allow

2 watch, feel, see, look at, hear, listen to / let, make, have

3 get

4 help

(C) 1 advises, to learn 2 saw, fly 3 hope, to be 4 heard, come 5 asked, to play 6 felt, blow 7 let, sleep 8 wanted, to draw 9 got, to cook 10 watched, run 11 listened to, speak 12 had, wash 13 helped, to wrap /wrap 14 made, do 15 let, fly

기본 TEST   p.58~61

 (A) 1 let, play 2 wanted, to come 3 made, feel 4 ordered, to do 5 watched, build 6 let, stay   7 saw, sleep   8 made, change   9 heard, catch   10 asked, to leave   11 help, water /to water   12 made, get   13 expects, to take   14 ordered, to be   15 felt, crawl

B 1 helps, (to) work   2 felt, need   3 had, clean   4 made, prepare   5 told, to meet   6 advised, to get   7 should have, get up ▶당신은 그가 6시까지 일어나도록 해야 합니다.   8 got, to paint   9 heard, show   10 saw, put out

C 1 saw, him, enter ▶지각동사는 원형부정사를 가집니다.   2 told, me, to study   3 felt, her, look at   4 heard, him, snore ▶지각동사는 원형부정사를 가집니다.   5 helped, me, (to) park   6 lets, her son, do   7 made, us, write   8 allowed, my daughter, to marry   9 wants, his son, to be   10 Let, them, go

D 1 had, her son, do   2 watched, the leaves, fall   3 allowed, me, to go   4 helps, her mom, (to) wash   5 let, me, watch ▶let-let-let   6 told, us, to bring   7 felt, a stranger, come ▶close:닫다. 가까이   8 made, her, change   9 let, us, play   10 heard, her, get

Unit 3
기초 TEST
p.63

A

1 her, eating something at night / 그녀가, 밤에 무언가를 먹는 것을
2 him, sneezing in the bathroom / 그가, 목욕탕에서 재채기하는 것을

3 the spider, coming down from the ceiling / 거미가, 천정으로부터 내려오는 것을
4 the sky, turning red / 하늘이, 붉게 변하는 것을
5 a bird, chirping in the backyard / 새가, 뒷마당에서 지저귀는 것을

1 his shoes, mended, 그의 신발을 수선시켰다 / John, to mend his shoes, John에게 그의 신발을 수선하게 했다(시켰다)
2 her hair, dyed, 그녀의 머리를 염색시켰다(염색하게 했다) / the hairdresser, dye her hair, 그 미용사에게 그녀의 머리를 염색하게 시켰다(했다)

기본 TEST
p.64~65

A 1 turn ▶내가 선풍기를 켜는 것은 능동. 사역동사 have가 있으므로 원형부정사 turn이 와야 합니다.   2 washed   3 stolen ▶steal-stole-stolen(과거분사)   4 checked ▶숙제를 검사 받는 것은 수동이므로 과거분사 checked가 와야 합니다.   5 to paint   6 repaired   7 polished   8 promoted ▶참모들이 승진된 것은 수동이므로 과거분사 promoted가 와야 합니다.   9 removed   10 waved

B 1 heard, her, singing/sing
2 saw, them, dancing/dance
3 felt, the bus, starting/start
4 got, her ears, pierced
▶그녀의 귀가 뚫린 것은 수동이므로 과거분사 pierced가 와야 합니다.
5 hear, the balloon, popping/pop
6 looked at, the sun, setting/set
7 had, his shirt, ironed ▶그의 셔츠가 다림질되어진 것은 수동이므로 과거분사 ironed가 와야 합니다.
8 had, the man, punished
▶남자가 처벌을 받은 것은 수동이므로 과거분사 punished가 와야 합니다.
9 got, me, to turn off
10 had, my hair, cut ▶cut-cut-cut

기초 TEST
p.67~69

A

1 her, not to go there / 그녀가, 거기에 가지 않기를
▶expect 기대하다 expectation 기대

2 me, not to get up late / 나에게, 늦게 일어나지 말라고

3 us, never to cross at the red light / 우리에게, 절대 빨간
불에 건너지 말라고

4 her, never to open the box / 그녀에게, 절대 그 상자를
열지 말라고

1 her not to climb
▶부정사의 부정은 부정사 앞에 not, never를 붙입니다.

2 us not to swim

3 the baby not to touch

4 her not to burn

5 me never to tell

B
1 c, e, b, a, d   2 a, b, g, d, e, c, f

C
1 to get   **2** find ▶had better+동사원형: **3** to
study   **4** act ▶may well+동사원형: ~하는 것은 당연하다.
5 jog   **6** keep ▶cannot but+동사원형   **7** fly   **8** to ask
9 to hide   **10** to exercise   **11** change   **12** to see
13 to mince   **14** obey   **15** be

기본 TEST
p.70~71

A
1 to return   **2** laugh   **3** to do   **4** say
5 do   **6** to look   **7** coming/come   **8** start   **9** to
eat   **10** sleep

B
1 not to tell   **2** had better take   **3** does
nothing but watch ▶do nothing but +동사원형   **4** not
to visit   **5** never to drink   **6** not to delay   **7** may
as well see   **8** may well be ▶may well+동사원형   **9**
cannot but agree   **10** not to catch

실력 TEST
p.72

A
1 To be frank with you
2 do nothing but rest
3 cannot but agree
4 Strange to say ▶형용사+to say: 말하기 ~하지만
5 to be honest ▶to be honest = to be frank with you
6 had better speak
7 may as well call
8 To tell the truth ▶close 가까운(형), 닫다(동)
9 may well say
10 so to speak

내신대비1
p.73~76

01 ①   02 ③   03 ④   04 ①   05 not   06 to
clean   07 steal   08 ③   09 ⑤   10 ⑤   11 ③,
④   12 to eat → eat   13 ①, ④   14 ②   15 to
not move → not to move   16 ③   17 ③
18 ②   19 ②, ⑤   20 stealing → stolen

01 want 목적어 to 동사원형: 목적어가 ~하기를 원하다

02 부정사의 부정은 부정사 앞에 not, never를 붙입니다.

03 지각동사는 원형부정사 또는 현재분사를 목적보어로 가집니다.
④ to say → say/saying

04 told를 제외한 let, had, made, saw는 원형부정사를 취합니다.

05 부정사의 부정은 부정사 앞에 not, never를 붙입니다.

06 help+목적어+to v-/v-(동사원형)

07 see+목적어+v(원형부정사)

08 ③ being cleaning → (to)be cleaned

09 make+목적어+동사원형 ① being → to be ② me go → me to go
③ her to go → her go ④ her dance → her to dance

10 have+목적어+원형부정사 → Joseph had me mow the lawn.

11 see+목적어+v-ing/v

12 let me to eat→let me eat / let+목적어+원형부정사

13 ①의 decide와 ④의 hope는 목적보어가 있는 5형식 문장을 만들 수
없습니다.

14 get+목적어+to부정사 → My father got me to water the garden.

15 부정사의 부정은 not+to+v 형태입니다.

16 부정사의 부정은 never+to+v 형태입니다.

17 머리카락이 파마가 되는 것은 수동이므로 과거분사 permed가 와야 합니다.

18 시계가 수리되는 것은 수동이므로 과거분사 repaired가 와야 합니다.

19 hear 목적어 v/v-ing

20 have+목적어+과거분사. 가방이 도난당한 것은 수동이므로 steal의 과거분사 stolen이 와야 합니다.

 내신대비2   p.77~80

01 ④   02 ③   03 ③   04 to be   05 ⑤   06 fixed
07 ①   08 let us play   09 ②   10 got, to play
11 stolen   12 ③   13 ④   14 ④   15 ②   16 ①
17 ①, ⑤   18 ④   19 calling, washed   20 ⑤

01 사역동사로 쓰인 make 이므로 원형부정사가 옵니다.
④ to open → open

02 사역동사로 쓰인 have 이므로 원형부정사가 옵니다.

03 ③ to be frank with you : 솔직하게 말해서

04 to 동사원형(to be)

06 자전거가 수리당하는 것이므로 과거분사(fixed)를 사용합니다.

07 사역동사로 쓰인 help는 to 부정사와 원형부정사 둘 다 사용 가능합니다.

08 사역동사로 쓰인 let 이므로 원형부정사가 옵니다. (let +목적격+동사원형)

09 ② to read → read

10 사역동사로 쓰인 get 은 to 부정사가 옵니다.

12 부정사의 부정은 not 이 부정사 앞에 옵니다.

13 ④ may well +동사원형

15 ~하지 않을 수 없다 ; cannot but 동사원형

16 ① told + 목적격 + to 부정사

17 hope 와 decide 는 목적보어가 있는 5형식 문장을 만들 수 없습니다.

20 to make matters worse ; 설상가상으로

 Chapter 3

동명사

Unit 1

기초 TEST   p.84~85

A

1 그 에세이를 읽어야 하는 것을, 그 에세이를 읽은 것을
▶forget to~: ~할 것을 잊다 / forget ~ing: ~한 것을 잊다

2 일하기 위해서, 일하는 것을

3 치우려고 노력했다, 시험 삼아 치워 보았다

4 방문한 것을, 방문해야 하는 것을

B   1 to close   2 dropping   3 to pull out
4 to meet   5 to buy   6 to climb   7 playing
8 drawing   9 to give   10 to call

기본 TEST   p.86~87

A   1 to lock   2 riding ▶try ~ing: 시험 삼아 해보다
3 living ▶remember ~ing: ~한 것을 기억하다   4 to get
5 to catch   6 to solve   7 to draw ▶stop to v-:
~하기 위해 멈추다   8 meeting   9 to fasten
10 to buy

B   1 forgot, wearing
2 try, pressing
3 remember, breaking
4 forget, to shave
5 stopped, drinking
6 try, to master
7 tried, jumping
8 stopped, watching
9 forgot, to take
10 remembers, to go

Unit 2

기초 TEST   p.89~91

A

1 노래하는 것을, 네가 노래하는 것을

2 요리하는 것을, Jane이 요리하는 것을

3 평상복 입는 것을, 그녀가 평상복 입는 것을

4 그녀의 아들이 영어를 잘 말하는 것을, 영어를 잘 말하는 것을

B 1 his(him) telling, telling

2 my(me) eating, eating

3 cooking, the chef's(the chef) cooking

4 collecting, his daughter's(his daughter) collecting

C 1 his(him), stealing

2 our(us), throwing

3 her, nagging

4 his(him), asking

5 our(us), sitting up ▶sit up over night: 밤을 새며 안 자다

6 his(him), starting

7 her, loving

8 the teacher's(the teacher), scolding

9 Mary's(Mary), advising

10 his(him) playing

기본 TEST   p.92~93

A 1 his(him) succeeding

2 Jane's(Jane) saying   3 playing

4 babies(babies') sleeping

5 his son's(his son) studying

6 his(him) getting   7 washing

8 her saying   9 her warning

10 becoming

B

1 포기하지 않는 것은   2 많이 알지 못하는 것을

3 더 오래 아프지 않는 것   4 그녀를 모르는 것이

5 선생님께 주목하지 않는 것은

---

1 Would you mind not opening the window?

2 He regrets not learning how to swim.
   ▶동명사의 부정은 동명사 앞에 not을 붙입니다.

3 There is no telling what will happen tomorrow.

4 Never going out at night is safe.

5 Not skipping breakfast helps to lose weight.
   ▶아침을 거르지 않는 것이 살을 빼는데 도움이 된다.

Unit 3

기초 TEST   p95

A 1 B 2 E 3 O 4 D 5 A 6 K 7 L 8 F
9 I 10 M 11 N 12 C 13 G 14 J 15 H

기본 TEST   p.96~97

A 1 draws 2 winning 3 getting 4 inviting
5 shopping 6 to buy 7 keeping 8 driving
9 drink 10 playing

B

1 is afraid of facing   2 will go fishing
3 are busy playing   4 feel like drinking
5 is bad(poor) at cooking
6 cannot help laughing
7 is looking forward to seeing
8 is worth reading   9 thanked her for helping
10 is proud of being

실력 TEST   p.98

A

1 was looking forward to meeting
2 feel like going   3 is worth learning
4 am afraid of going   5 went hiking
6 is busy studying
7 spends 2 hours watching
8 cannot help putting   9 is good at playing
10 is fond of talking

내신대비1 p.99~102

> 01 ② 02 ⑤ 03 ③ 04 ③ 05 like 06 of
> 07 ③ 08 shopping 09 ⑤ 10 ④
> 11 my(me) 12 ③ 13 ② 14 ① 15 ③
> 16 ⑤ 17 ② 18 ② 19 ③ 20 ⑤

01 B의 대답을 보면 전화를 아직 하지 않았다는 것을 알 수 있기에 remember to v: ~할 것을 기억하다 가 맞는 표현입니다.

02 동명사의 의미상의 주어는 소유격이나 목적격으로 나타냅니다.

03 동명사의 부정은 동명사 앞에 not을 붙입니다.

04 cannot help ~ing: ~하지 않을 수 없다

05 feel like ~ing: ~하고 싶다

06 be proud of ~ing: ~한 것을 자랑스러워하다

07 spend 시간 ~ing: ~하는 데 시간을 보내다

08 be fond of ~ing: ~하는 것을 좋아하다

09 ① to play → playing ② take → taking ③ to see → seeing ④ meeting → to meet

10 be afraid of ~ing: ~를 두려워하다, ~을 걱정하다

11 동명사의 의미상의 주어는 소유격이나 목적격으로 나타내므로 my 또는 me가 와야 합니다.

12 ③ good at draw → good at drawing / be good at ~ing: ~을 잘하다

13 enjoy ~ing: ~을 하는 것을 즐기다

14 ② to → at ③ on → in ④ in → of ⑤ to → of

17 ② in playing → like playing / feel like ~ing: ~하고 싶다

18 동명사의 부정은 동명사 앞에 not이나 never가 옵니다.

19 be busy ~ing: ~하느라 바쁘다

20 thank A for ~ing: ~한 것에 대해 A에게 감사하다

내신대비2 p.103~106

> 01 ⑤ 02 ③ 03 to forget 04 visiting 05 ①
> 06 ④ 07 ① 08 ① 09 ③ 10 ⑤ 11 ⑤
> 12 ③ 13 supporting 14 doing 15 ②
> 16 his(him) 17 ⑤ 18 ② 19 ④ 20 ③

01 동명사의 의미상의 주어는 소유격 또는 목적격을 사용합니다.

02 stop ~ing ; ~하던 것을 멈추었다

03 대개, 아직 못한 것은 to 부정사, 이미 한 것은 동명사 사용합니다.

05 전치사 다음에는 명사(대명사) 또는 동명사를 사용합니다.

08 의미상의 주어가 일반적인 사람일 경우 대개 생략합니다.

09 ③ she → her

10 ⑤ being → be

12 plan to ~ , 나머지들은 모두 동명사를 사용합니다.

14 be busy ~ing ; ~하느라고 바쁘다

15 be worth ~ing ; ~할 가치가 있다

17 forget to ~ ; ~할 것을 잊다, forget ~ing ; ~ 한 것을 잊다.

18 looked forward to ~ing ; ~하는 것을 고대했다.
  이때의 to 는 전치사입니다. ② meet → meeting

Chapter 4

분사구문

Unit 1

기초 TEST p.109

A **1** 먹고 난 후에 ▶After he has dinner **2** 비록 보았을지라도 ▶Though she saw her daughter **3** 서두른다면 ▶If we hurry up **4** 한 후에 **5** 몸이 약하기 때문에 **6** 목이 말라서 **7** 살이 찌므로 **8** 연 후에 **9** 운전하면서 **10** 켠 후에 ▶After she turned on the TV

기본 TEST p.110~111

A **1** 다녔을 때 **2** 자고 있는 동안에 ▶소파에서 자고 있는 동안에 Anne은 좋은 꿈을 꿨다. **3** 만난다면 **4** 만날지라도 **5** 빗은 후에 ▶매일 아침 그녀의 머리를 빗은 후에 그녀는 학교에 간다. **6** 살고 있으므로 **7** 휘파람을 불면서 ▶While Tommy whistles merrily **8** 일지라도 ▶그녀는 10살일지라도 영자 신문을 읽을 수 있다. **9** 하기 때문에 **10** 머무는 동안에

B **1** 깼기 때문에, 원인 **2** 듣는다면, 조건 ▶If he hears her news **3** 날아가면서, 동시동작 ▶While the magpie flew away from the branch **4** 가졌을지라도, 양보 **5** 빌려준 후에, 시간 ▶After she lent some money to Jane **6** 받는다면, 조건 **7** 잃어버렸기 때문에, 원인 ▶Since she lost the car key **8** 흔들면서, 동시동작 **9** 건널 때, 시간 **10** 시끄럽게 떠들었기 때문에, 원인 ▶Because they made a noise in class

Unit 2

기초 TEST   p.113

A

1 When I, Solving the math quiz
  ▶나는 수학 문제를 풀 때, 머리가 아프다.

2 While we, Doing our homework
  ▶우리의 숙제를 하면서, 우리는 너무 많이 얘기한다.

3 Because he, Exercising everyday

4 While she, Taking a shower
  ▶그녀는 샤워를 하면서 크게 노래를 불렀다.

5 When they, Riding a bus

6 When he, Going out of his office

7 As it, Growing up

기본 TEST   p.114~118

A

1 When I, Watching ▶영화를 볼 때, 나는 팝콘을 많이 먹는다.

2 Because he, Loving

3 As she, Losing
  ▶그녀는 가방을 잃어버렸으므로, 돈이 하나도 없었다.

4 After I, Finishing ▶숙제를 끝낸 후에, 나는 게임을 할 것이다.

5 Though I, Being

6 As he, Being

7 After she, Turning off

8 Because he, Being

9 When I, Going
  ▶나는 조깅을 하러 갈 때, 나의 개를 데려갈 것이다.

10 Though she, Being
  ▶비록 그녀가 유명한 가수였지만, 그녀는 행복하지 않았다.

B

1 If you, Reading many good books

2 When I, Taking photos
  ▶나는 사진을 찍을 때 내 왼쪽 눈을 감는다.

3 Though she, Being a miser

4 When I, Fixing my computer

5 After they, Playing soccer under the sun
  ▶태양 아래서 축구를 한 뒤, 그들은 그늘에서 쉰다.

6 If you, Going straight

7 As he, Slipping on the ice
  ▶얼음 위에 미끄러져서 그는 아팠다.

8 While she, Taking a walk ▶take a walk 산책하다

9 As he, Selling all the fruits
  ▶그는 과일을 다 팔았으므로 집으로 돌아갔다.

10 Because he, Being late for school
  ▶그는 학교에 지각했기 때문에 선생님에게 혼이 났다.

Unit 3

기초 TEST   p.118~119

A

1 Mr. Brown, he / Sneaking up, Mr. Brown ▶그의 여
  동생에게 살금살금 다가갔을 때, Mr. Brown은 그녀를 놀라게 했다.

2 Tom, he / Running, Tom
  ▶평소처럼 달리면, Tom은 경주를 이길 것이다.

3 my friend, she / Being, my friend
  ▶내 친구는 비록 키는 작지만, 똑똑하다.

4 dad, he / Eating, dad

5 Mary, she / Hearing, Mary
  ▶Mary는 알람을 듣고, 일어났다.

6 it, they, It being ▶비가 와서, 그들은 콘서트를 취소했다.

7 it, we, It being

B

1 Jane, she / Turning off, Jane

2 he, he / Studying, he

3 it, we / It being, we

4 the mice, they / Seeing, the mice

5 plastic, it / Being, plastic
  ▶플라스틱은 가벼울지라도, 단단하다.

6 he, he / Washing, he ▶그는 설거지를 하면서 음악을 들었다.

7 my sister, she / Finding, my sister
  ▶나의 여동생이 그녀의 개를 찾는다면, 그녀는 기쁠 것이다.

8 she, she / Being, she

9 Bill, he / Having, Bill

> Bill은 저녁을 먹으면서, 그는 뉴스를 본다.

10 she, she / Getting, she

> 그녀는 생일에 선물을 받아서 행복했다.

기본 TEST
p.120~121

 A 1 Being too busy, Too busy

2 Shopping with mom, When shopping with mom

3 Being so frightened, So frightened

> 그녀는 너무 두려워서, 그녀의 방에 숨었다.

4 Wrapping the CD, While wrapping the CD

5 Finding my ring again

> 반지를 다시 찾으면, 나는 그것을 빼지 않을 것이다.

B

1 being hot, 현재 ▶지금 더워서, 그는 그의 외투를 벗을 것이다.

2 Running, 진행

> 기차를 잡기 위해 뛰느라, 그는 표지판을 보지 못했다.

3 Walking, 진행 ▶그녀는 길을 걸으면서, 조용히 웃었다.

4 Being covered, covered, 현재

> 눈으로 덮여서, 오르기가 힘들다.

5 Combing, 진행

> Eli는 그녀의 머리카락을 빗질하며 어머니에게 아침을 달라고 부탁했다.

6 Filled, Being filled, 현재

7 Eating, 진행

> Maria가 무언가를 먹을 때, 그녀는 벨이 울리는 소리를 들었다.

8 Taking, 진행 ▶그는 샤워를 하면서, 기쁨을 느꼈다.

9 Being sick, Sick, 과거

10 Being so tall, So tall, 과거

> 키가 너무 커서, 그녀는 허리를 굽혀야 했다.

실력 TEST
p.122~124

 A 1 Before ▶그녀는 밖에 나가기 전에, 불을 끈다.

2 x   3 Before   4 x ▶너무 바쁠 때, 나는 전화를 받지 않는다.

5 x   6 Before   7 Before ▶Julia는 티셔츠를 사기 전에, 항상
입어 본다.   8 Before ▶접속사 before는 생략하지 않습니다.

1 Not making ▶실수를 하지 않아서, 그는 약간의 용돈을 받았다.

2 Not having

3 Never watching

> 뉴스를 전혀 보지 않아서, 아빠는 바깥 세상에 관해 아무 것도 알지 못한다.

4 Not practicing ▶ruin 망치다

5 Not wearing ▶머플러를 하지 않아서, 그는 인후염에 걸렸다.

B

1 Before getting ▶운동을 하기 전에, 그는 약간의 물을 마신다.

2 (Being) covered

3 Before forgetting

4 Looking at

5 Before going ▶밖에 나가기 전에, 그녀는 거울을 본다.

6 Before making

7 Before leaving

8 Forgetting

> 개한테 밥을 주는 것을 잊으면, 그들은 미안함을 느낄 것이다.

9 Before believing

10 Playing

> 그는 비디오 게임을 하고 있었기 때문에, 나에게 대답을 하지 않았다.

C

1 While doing, Doing ▶우리는 숙제를 하면서, 간식을 먹는다.

2 After walking, Walking

3 While taking, Taking

4 Being bored, Bored

> 분사구문에서 being은 생략이 가능합니다.

5 Eating ▶Bill은 뷔페에서 너무 많이 먹어서, 배가 아팠다.

6 Exercising

> 우리가 운동을 열심히 하면, 우리는 옷이 젖게 될 것이다.

01 ④　02 ②　03 ③　04 Not following
05 ③　06 ③　07 ①　08 Be →Being / 생략
09 he → Jimmy　10 ②,③　11 ①　12 ①
13 ③　14 ⑤　15 Not preparing　16 ①
17 he is an athlete　18 ②　19 ④　20 (While) Waiting for the vacation

01 목욕을 할 때, 나는 음악을 듣습니다.
02 분사구문의 부정이 not 분사 앞에 옵니다.
03 접속사 before는 생략할 수 없습니다.
04 분사구문의 부정은 not이 분사 앞에 옵니다.
05 분사구문을 만들 때 주절의 주어인 he를 부사절의 주어 고유명사 (Mike)로 바꾸어 주어야 주어가 정확히 누구인지 알 수 있습니다.
06 창문을 열고, Christie는 예쁜 새를 발견했습니다.
07 ① Because being tired → Being tired
　　Because는 분사구문에서 생략합니다.
08 분사구문에서 동사 be는 being으로 바꿔 주거나 또는 생략 합니다.
09 분사구문을 만들 때 주절의 주어인 he를 고유명사 Jimmy로 바꾸어 줘야 주어가 정확히 누구인지 알 수 있습니다.
10 ② 나는 하얀 치마를 입고 있을 때, 아이스크림을 먹고 싶습니다.
　　Being wearing → Wearing / When wearing
　　③ before는 생략하지 않습니다.
11 분사구문의 부정은 not이나 never를 분사 앞에 넣으면 됩니다.
13 분사구문의 부정은 'Not+분사'입니다.
15 회의를 잘 준비하지 못해서, 나는 좋은 기회를 놓쳤습니다.
16 부사절의 동사가 진행형인 경우 being은 생략합니다.

01 ③　02 ①　03 ②　04 Traveling　05 Kate
06 It　07 ①,③　08 ③,⑤　09 ①　10 ⑤
11 ②　12 ④　13 ③　14 ③　15 Not knowing
16 ③　17 ②　18 ①　19 ①　20 ④

02 was의 동사원형은 be 이므로 Being 이 옵니다.
05 부사절의 주어(Kate)가 명사이므로 주절의 주어(she)를 Kate 로 바꾸어 주어야 합니다.
06 비인칭 주어 it 은 주절의 주어(he)와 다르므로 그대로 남겨둡니다.
07 though 가 이끄는 부사절을 분사구문으로 바꿀 때, 그대로 남겨두기도 합니다.

08 수동태의 분사구문 시 being 은 생략 가능합니다.
09 접속사 before는 분사구문 시 생략하지 않습니다.
10 접속사 because는 분사구문 시 생략합니다.
11 분사구문의 부정은 not 이 맨 앞으로 나옵니다.
13 진행형의 분사구문 시 being 은 생략합니다.③ Being drinking → Drinking
17 시제가 과거(had to take)이므로 Being 이 과거(was)로 되돌아가야 합니다.
19 접속사 before는 분사구문 시 생략하지 않습니다.
20 분사구문의 부정은 not 이 맨 앞으로 나옵니다.

Chapter 5

조동사

Unit 1

기초 TEST　　p.139~141

A

1 볼 수 있다, 볼 수 있었다, 볼 수 있었다, 볼 수 있을 것이다
　▶ can, be able to, could, will be able to
2 일해야만 할 것이다, 일해야만 한다, 일해야만 했다, 일해야만 한다
　▶ must = have to /has to

1 could, will be able to, can, was / were able to
2 will have to, must, had to, have / has to

B　1 could, was able to　▶ could=was/were able to
2 had to　3 had to　4 had to　5 Were they able to, Could they

1 will be able to　2 will have to　3 will have to
4 will be able to　5 will be able to

C　1 could pick, was able to pick
2 had to drive
3 could make, was able to make
4 had to sow
5 had to speak
6 was able to do, could do
7 were able to get, could get
　▶ they가 복수이므로 was가 아닌 were able to가 옳은 표현입니다.
8 was able to make, could make

A　1 will be able to do

2 will have to apologize　3 will be able to use

4 will have to answer　5 will be able to do

6 will have to hear　7 will be able to do

8 will have to keep　9 will be able to finish

10 will have to face

 B　1 You will have to get

2 She could care (She was able to care)

3 Carol had to wear

4 Ants will have to work

5 The tiger will be able to catch

6 She had to keep

7 You will be able to do

8 Tony was able to cut (Tony could cut)

9 Nancy had to wait

10 The police will be able to arrest

Unit 2

A　1 8　2 3　3 5　4 6, 7　5 4　6 1　7 2

B　1 used to+동사 원형　2 used to+동사 원형

3 may well+동사 원형　4 had better+동사 원형

5 would rather+동사 원형　6 get used to~ing

7 (be) used to~ing　8 may as well+동사 원형

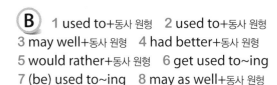 **C**　1 used to walk (would walk) ▶과거의 습관

2 is used to washing

3 may well cry

4 get used to waiting

5 would rather take

6 used to be ▶과거에 카페가 있었으나 지금은 없는 상태

7 used to see (would see)

8 may well get

9 had better catch

10 would rather talk

 A　1 used to play (would play)

2 may as well do

3 used to be

4 may well be

5 is used to teaching

　▶현재 그녀는 음악을 가르치는 것에 익숙하다.

6 got used to using

　▶Jim은 내 컴퓨터를 쓰는 것에 익숙해졌다.

7 would rather leave

8 had better stop

9 may well turn

10 used to go (would go)

　▶우리는 가끔 하이킹을 가곤했습니다.

내신대비1　　　　　　　　　p.149~152

01 과거 : Jim could(was able to) understand it soon. 미래 : Jim will be able to understand it soon.　02 과거 : Sumi had to do her homework. 미래: Sumi will have to do her homework.

03 ④　04 ③　05 ③　06 ④　07 had to stop

08 could, was able to　09 ①　10 ②

11 could, was able to　12 will be able to

13 will have to　14 taking → take　15 ⑤

16 ④　17 taking → take　18 ②　19 may as well put　20 may well be

01 can의 과거형은 could, was/were able to, 미래형은 will be able to.

02 must의 과거형은 had to, 미래형은 will have to.

03 could=was/were able to, Tommy는 단수이므로 was가 와야 합니다.

04 ③ will able to → will be able to

06 ① were → was ② coulds → could ③ keeps → keep ⑤ gets → get

08 can의 과거형은 could, was/were able to

09 will be able to: ~할 수 있을 것이다 will have to: ~해야만 할 것이다

10 ①③④⑤의 could는 능력, ②의 could는 허락을 구하는 공손한 요청의 표현입니다.

11 could, was able to: ~할 수 있었다

12 will be able to: ~할 수 있을 것이다

13 will have to: ~해야만 할 것이다

14 had better+동사원형이므로 taking이 아닌 take가 올바른 표현입니다.

15 ① asking → ask ② to drink → drink ③ going → go
④ cooking → cook

16 was/were able to=could

17 'had to + 동사원형'이므로 taking이 아닌 take가 와야 합니다.

18 will have to: ~해야 할 것이다.

19 may as well 동사원형: ~하는 것이 좋겠다.

20 may well 동사원형: ~하는 것이 당연하다

내신대비2   p.153~156

01 ③ 02 ③ 03 ⑤ 04 will be able to 05 ④
06 ② 07 ③ 08 ① 09 ⑤ 10 ① 11 ④
12 ⑤ 13 may well like 14 Must 15 You will
get used to doing your work 16 ① 17 could
understand (= was able to understand) 18 will
be able to understand 19 ① 20 ③

03 ⑤ may ~ ; ~해도 좋다/~일지도 모른다

04 will can은 사용하지 않습니다.
can의 미래형은 will be able to입니다.

06 must ~(~해야 만 한다) 의 과거형은 had to ~ 입니다

08 would rather A than B ; B 하느니 차라리 A 하는게 낫겠다

09 get used to ~ing ; ~하는 데 익숙해지다

10 used to 동사원형 ; 동작은 would로 바꾸어 쓸 수 있으나,
상태는 바꾸어 쓸 수 없습니다.

11 ④ cook → cooking

13 may well 동사원형 ;~하는 것은 당연하다

14 대답이 must 이므로, 질문도 must 가 옳습니다.

17 can 의 과거형; could 또는 was(were) able to ~

18 can 의 미래형; will be able to ~

20 ③ will able to → will be able to

Chapter 6

수동태

Unit 1

기초 TEST   p.159~161

A

1 길러졌다, 길러진다, 길러질 것입니다
2 구워질 것입니다, 구워진다, 구워졌다

1 will be, was, is **2** was, is, will be **3** is, was,
will be

B **1** was called **2** will be counted **3** are
washed **4** was robbed **5** were soaked **6** will
be changed **7** were rescued **8** was cut **9** will
be televised **10** is scheduled

C

1 was made, 과거 / will be made, 미래 / is made, 현재
2 will be invited, 미래/ was invited, 과거 / is invited,
현재
3 was seen, 과거 / is seen, 현재 / will be seen 미래
▶see-saw-seen

기본 TEST   p.162~163

A **1** designed, was designed
2 will throw, will be thrown ▶throw-threw-thrown
3 solved, were solved
4 comforts, is comforted
5 removed, were removed
6 hunt, are hunted ▶물개들은 돌고래들에 의해 사냥된다.
7 will shovel, will be shoveled
8 separated, were separated

9 touched, were touched
　▶많은 사람들이 그 영화에 의해 감동을 받았다.
10 will amaze, will be amazed

B 1 will make, will be made
2 sells, is sold ▶sell—sold—sold
3 hangs up, is hung up
4 folded, was folded
5 will knit, will be knitted
6 opened, was opened
7 received, were received
8 will select, will be selected
9 stung, was stung ▶그의 손은 벌에 의해 쏘였다.
10 polished, were polished

Unit 2

1 만들어질 수 있다, 만들어질지도 모른다, 만들어져야 한다
2 구워지고 있는 중이다, 구워지고 있는 중이었다, 다 구워졌다

1 is being chased, may be chased, has been
　chased
2 has been published, must be published

1 may be delivered　　2 is being produced
3 has been erased　　4 may be helped
5 have been eaten ▶eat—ate—eaten
6 can be packed　　7 is being played
8 has been moved　　9 was being performed
10 has to be taken ▶조동사(has to)의 수동태입니다.

B
1 must be cooked/ 조동사, is being cooked/ 진행형,
　has been cooked/ 현재완료
2 was being tuned/ 진행형, has been tuned/ 현재완료,
　must be tuned/ 조동사
　▶피아노는 조율사에 의해 조율되어야 합니다.
3 are being made/ 진행형, have been made/ 현재완료,
　may be made/ 조동사
　▶some sandwiches는 복수이므로 has가 아닌 have가 와야 합니다.

A 1 is keeping, is being kept
2 can hit, can be hit
3 have done, has been done
4 can win, can be won
5 is repairing, is being repaired
6 must weed, must be weeded
7 have drilled, has been drilled
8 are sweeping, is being swept
　▶sweep—swept—swept
9 must send, must be sent
10 have built, has been built

B 1 may remember, may be remembered
2 has bitten, has been bitten ▶bite—bit—bitten
3 is writing, is being written
4 can break, can be broken
5 have built, has been built
6 was grilling, were being grilled
7 should read, should be read
8 is cutting, is being cut
9 were singing, was being sung ▶sing—sang—sung
10 have to take, have to be taken
　▶vitamins는 복수이므로 have가 와야 합니다.

Unit 3

A 1 him, He, was given a sweater

2 me, I, was given a pen

3 them, they, were shown a necklace

4 us, we, are taught P.E.

5 me, I, was told her love story

1 pork, Pork, was cooked, us

2 some cookies, Some cookies, are sent, us

3 a memo, A memo, will be written, Paul

4 a story book, A story book, is read, me

5 a ruler, A ruler, was passed, Tom

B 1 to   2 to   3 to   4 to   5 to   6 for

▶make+for   7 to   8 to   9 for ▶buy+for   10 for

11 to   12 to   13 for   14 to   15 of ▶ask+of

A

1 was given, a pen, by him / was given, to me, by him

2 are taught, math, by her / is taught, to us, by her ▶teach+to

3 was passed, to him, by her

4 was made, for me, by my auntie

5 will be shown, her painting, by Jane / will be shown, to him, by Jane ▶그는 Jane에 의해 그녀의 그림을 보게 될 것입니다. / 그녀의 그림은 Jane에 의해 그에게 보여질 것입니다.

6 was bought, for her, by him
   ▶buy는 직접목적어만을 주어로 쓰는 동사입니다.

7 were given, some food, by Jimmy / was given, to them, by Jimmy

8 was cooked, for us, by mom

1 her son, Her son, was made a musician
   ▶그녀의 아들은 그녀에 의해 음악가가 되었다.

2 the baby, The baby, was named Sally
   ▶아기가 그들에 의해 Sally라고 이름 지어졌습니다.

3 the river, The river, is called 'Han-kang'

4 him, He, is believed generous
   ▶그는 나에게 자상하다고 믿어진다.

5 the ceiling, The ceiling was painted white
   ▶천장이 Jimmy에 의해 하얀 색으로 칠해졌다.

1 him, He, was seen, to enter the house
   ▶그는 나에 의해 집에 들어오는 것이 목격되었다.

2 her, She, was heard, to come closer ▶see, hear와 같은 지각동사의 목적보어로 쓰인 원형부정사는 수동태에서는 to부정사로 바뀝니다.

3 him, He, was made, to do his homework
   ▶사역동사의 목적보어로 쓰인 원형부정사는 to부정사로 바뀝니다.

4 his brother, His brother, is helped, to do the laundry work

5 him, He, is made to act like a gentleman

1 the board, The board, was colored, green, by the girl

2 the sea, The sea, is called, 'the Pacific', by them

3 us, We, are made, to write a book report, by the teacher

4 him, He, was made, tired, by the assignment

5 the story, The story, was found, false, by Bob.
   ▶그 이야기는 Bob에 의해 거짓인 것으로 밝혀졌다.

6 the wind, The wind, was felt, to blow hard, by Jane

7 Obama, Obama, was elected President, by Americans

8 him, He, is made, upset, by her

9 me, I, am helped, to finish the work, by dad
   ▶사역동사의 목적보어로 쓰인 원형부정사는 to부정사로 바뀝니다.

10 the kitten, The kitten, was named, 'Ming-Ming', by Brian and Kate.

D

1 him, He, was made, to stop it, by her.

2 him, He, is considered, a professor by her

3 a trendy tie, A trendy tie, was bought, for him, by me. ▶trendy 유행하는, trend 유행

4 her, She, was helped, to escape, by them.

5 the door, The door, was left, open, by Tom.

6 Paul, Paul, was found, good, by her.

7 her, She, was made, to cry, by us
   ▶사역동사(make, help)의 목적보어로 쓰인 원형부정사는 to부정사로 바뀝니다.

8 students, Students, were seen, to study in the library, by Jenny.
   ▶지각동사의 목적보어로 쓰인 원형부정사는 to부정사로 바뀝니다.

9 him, He, was made, sad, by the news.

10 the man, The man, was found, homeless, by us.

Unit 4

기초 TEST
p.179

A 1 with / at 2 in 3 with 4 with 5 with
6 to 7 with 8 at(by) 9 with 10 of 11 about
12 of / from 13 at 14 in ▶He was involved in a crime. 그는 범죄에 연관되었습니다.

기본 TEST
p.180~181

A 1 with 2 with 3 about 4 in 5 with
6 of 7 at(by) 8 to 9 at 10 with(at) 11 with
12 of 13 with 14 in ▶Tom은 사건에 관련되어 있습니다.

B 1 isn't interested in 2 are surprised at(by)
3 is tired of 4 was worried about ▶safety 안전, safe 안전한 5 am satisfied with ▶present (형)현재의, (명)선물,

현재 6 is tired with ▶housework=house chores 7 are made from 8 is filled with 9 are made of
10 is disappointed at

실력 TEST
p.182

A 1 is crowded with 2 is known to 3 is covered with 4 is filled with 5 be involved in
6 are pleased with(at) 7 are worried about 8 is interested in 9 is made of 10 are surprised at(by) ▶all of + 복수명사 다음에는 복수 동사가 와야 합니다.

내신대비1
p.183~186

01 ② 02 ④ 03 ③ 04 is being built by dad 05 ② 06 been 07 ③ 08 ② 09 ②
10 ④ 11 ⑤ 12 ① 13 about 14 at
15 with(at) 16 ③ 17 ④ 18 to play the piano 19 A bag, for him 20 ④

01 An essay는 단수이므로 동사 is, write의 과거 분사 written이 와야 합니다.

02 broke는 과거 시제이므로 be 동사 was와 과거 분사 broken이 와야 합니다.

03 미래 시제 수동태: will+be+P.P

04 is being built: 만들어지고 있는 중이다.

05 조동사 should 다음에는 동사원형이 와야 합니다. ② been → be

07 ③ checking → checked

08 give는 전치사 to와 함께 합니다.

09 ② to this cap → this cap

10 ④에 쓰인 동사 buy는 직접목적어만을 주어로 합니다.

11 조동사의 수동태는 '조동사+be+P.P'

12 Josh는 우리에 의해 리더로 선출이 된 것이므로 수동태로 표현하고/누군가 내 차를 훔쳐간 것이므로 능동태로 나타내야 합니다.

13 be worried about: ~에 대해 걱정하다

14 be surprised at: ~에 대해 놀라다

15 be pleased with(at): ~로 즐겁다

16 be tired of: ~에 싫증나다

17 지각동사의 목적보어로 쓰인 원형부정사는 to부정사로 바뀝니다.

18 지각동사의 목적보어로 쓰인 원형부정사는 to부정사로 바뀝니다.

19 동사 buy는 전치사 for를 간접목적어와 함께 씁니다.

내신대비2   p.187~190

01 ④   02 ②   03 ⑤   04 playing → played
05 ④   06 ⑤   07 ②   08 ④   09 ③
10 to go out   11 ⑤   12 ④   13 ⑤   14 was advised to take a break   15 ④   16 ⑤   17 ⑤
18 Dad/honey/mom   19 ③   20 seen to

01 수동태 과거 ; was(were) + p.p. + by 목적격

03 수동태 미래 ; will be + p.p. + by 목적격

04 진행형의 수동태 ; be동사 + being +p.p. + by 목적격

05 조동사의 수동태 ; 조동사 + be +p.p. + by 목적격

06 현재완료의 수동태 ; have(has) + been +p.p. + by 목적격

09 4형식 문장에서 make(만들어 주다)의 수동태에서는
전치사 for +목적격이 됩니다.

10 지각동사 see의 수동태에서는 to가 다시 살아납니다.

11 4형식 문장에서 ask(물어보다)의 수동태에서는
전치사 of +목적격이 됩니다.

12 ④ 사역동사 have는 수동태로 바꾸어 쓰지 않습니다.

13 ⑤ be interested in ~ ; ~에 흥미가 있다

16 send/pass/read/write 등의 동사는 간접목적어를 주어로 하여
수동태 문장을 만들지 않습니다.

17 ⑤ from → with

20 지각동사 see의 수동태에서는 to가 다시 살아납니다.

Chapter 7

완료

Unit 1

기초 TEST   p.194~195

A

1 계속 있다, 가버렸다, 가 본적이 있다

2 가 본적이 있다, 계속 있다, 가버렸다

1 has gone to, has been to, has been in

2 has been to, has been in, has gone to

B   **1** been to ▶나는 전에 재즈 축제에 가 본 적이 있습니다.(경험)

2 been to ▶당신은 중국에 가 본 적이 있습니까? 1인칭/2인칭 주어
(I/we/you)는 have gone to(가 버렸다)와 함께 쓸 수 없습니다.

3 gone to ▶Jack은 L.A.로 가버렸습니다.

4 been to

5 been in ▶우리는 아침 7시부터 사무실에 계속 있습니다.

6 gone to

7 been in

8 been to ▶우리는 그의 사무실에 세 번 가 봤습니다.(경험)

9 gone to ▶그들은 Tom을 만나기 위해 카페로 가버렸습니다.

10 been in ▶Jinho는 공부를 하기 위해 시드니에 계속 있습니다.

11 been to

12 been in

13 been in
▶나는 지난 주 목요일부터 친구의 집에 계속 머물고 있습니다.

14 gone to ▶그는 그의 고향으로 가버렸습니다.

15 been in

기본 TEST   p.196~197

A

1 has gone to   **2** has been in

3 has been to   **4** have been in

5 has been to   **6** has gone to

7 has been in   **8** have gone to

9 has been to ▶state: 주(미국, 스위스 같은 국가는 여러 개의 주로
이루어진 연방 국가입니다.)

10 have been to

 B

1 has been to	**2** has gone to
3 has gone to	**4** has been in
5 has been to	**6** has been in
7 have, been to	**8** has, been in
9 have been in	**10** has gone to

Unit 2

기초 TEST   p.199

 A   **1** have been reading, had read

2 has been teaching, had taught

3 had watched, has been watching

4 had visited, have been visiting

5 have been working, had worked

기본 TEST   p.200

 A   **1** has been making

2 have been looking

3 has loved

4 has been using

5 have known

6 had spent, had ▶돈을 과거(돈이 없었음) 이전에 다 써버렸으
므로 과거완료 had spent가 와야 합니다.

7 told, had gone

8 knew, had read

9 saw, started

10 had baked, smelled

 내신대비1   p.201~204

01 ①   **02** ④   **03** ⑤   **04** gone → been
05 has been taking   **06** ④   **07** ③   **08** ⑤
09 have known   **10** ④   **11** has been to
Seoul three times   **12** ③   **13** ③   **14** ④
15 ②   **16** ⑤   **17** Have you been to   **18** ⑤
19 ④   **20** ⑤

01 have/has been to: ~에 가 본 적이 있습니다 (경험)

02 has/have been in: ~에 계속 있습니다, ~에서 지내고 있습니다

03 has/have gone to: ~로 가 버렸다, ~로 가고 없습니다(결과)

04 gone → been, 경험을 나타낼 때는 been이 와야 합니다.

06 ① be → been ② have → has ③ have studying → have studied
⑤ play → playing

07 해석: Tommy는 나무를 심고 있습니다. / 그들은 2007년부터 서울
에 계속 있습니다.

08 나의 남동생은 학교로 가서 지금 집에 없으므로 has gone to the
school

09 우리가 10대였을 때 나는 그를 캠프에서 만났다. 그 때부터, 우리는
서로를 알고 지냈습니다. 현재에도 계속되고 있는 '상태'이므로 현재
완료를 사용한다.

10 현재완료 진행형은 (have/has +been +~ing)입니다.

11 has been to: 가 본 적이 있다.

12 선물을 받은 것이 앞선 시제이므로 과거완료를, 잃어버린 것이 나중
시제이므로 과거로 나타냅니다.

13 Andy는 30분 전부터 버스를 기다리기 시작해서 아직도 기다리고
있습니다.

14 너는 공원에 가 본 적이 있니? (have been to: 경험)

15 프로젝트를 끝낸 다음(과거완료) 점심을 먹으러 나간 것입니다.(과
거) 과거완료 had completed가 맞는 표현입니다.

16 어제 샀던(과거완료-had bought), 그녀에게 줬다(과거-gave)

17 경험을 물을 때는 have been to를 사용합니다.

18 그녀는 캐나다로 떠난 것이므로 has gone 이 와야 합니다.

19 ④ knowing → know, know는 상태를 나타내는 동사이므로 현재
완료진행형을 사용하지 않습니다.

20 ⑤ He had called her once before Liz moved to LA. / Liz가 LA로
이사를 가기 전에(과거) 그가 그녀에게 전화를 했습니다.(과거완료)

내신대비2
p.205~208

01 ③　02 ④　03 ⑤　04 ②　05 at/in　06 ①
07 ⑤　08 ④　09 ⑤　10 ①　11 ④　12 has
been sleeping　13 have known　14 has been to
15 had broken　16 ③　17 has been to North
Korea twice　18 has been eating　19 ③　20 ④

01 ~에 가 본적이 있다 ; have(has) been to ~

02 ~에 가 버렸다 ; have(has) gone to ~

03 ~에서 지내고 있다 ; have(has) been in(at) ~

05 대개 넓은 장소(도시 또는 그 이상)에서는 전치사 in,
　　좁은 장소에서는 at을 사용합니다.

06 주어가 1인칭/2인칭의 경우는 'have(has) gone to ~ '를 사용 할
　　수 없습니다.

08 과거시제가 2개 일 때, 더 과거(대 과거)에는 대개 'had + p.p'를
　　사용합니다

09 현재완료진행형 ; have(has) + been + ~ing
　　동작동사로 과거에 하기 시작하여 현재(지금)도 하고 있음을 나타냅니다.

10 현재완료진행형 ; have(has) + been + ~ing

13 상태동사 know 는 현재완료진행형을 사용하지 않습니다.

15 과거시제가 2개 일 때, 더 과거(대 과거)에는 대개 'had + p.p'를
　　사용합니다

18 동작동사 eat 의 현재완료진행형입니다.

19 과거시제가 2개 일 때, 더 과거(대 과거)에는 대개 'had + p.p'를
　　사용합니다

20 대답이 No, I haven't. 이므로 질문도 현재완료 형태(Have you ~ ?)
　　이어야 합니다.

종/합/문/제 1
p.210~215

01 ④　02 ⑤　03 of you　04 ③　05 for him
→ of him　06 swimming　07 ③　08 ③
09 ②　10 have → having　11 (Being) Too
sick　12 ④　13 had to　14 could(=was able
to)　15 will have to finish　16 will be able to
cook　17 ⑤　18 ④　19 ②　20 ③　21 ⑤
22 too full to　23 ①　24 ②　25 was built

01 It~to의 형태에서 부정사 바로 앞에 for+목적격(him)을 써서 의미
　　상의 주어를 나타냅니다.

02 remember ~ing: ~한 것을 기억하다

03 사람을 칭찬하는 형용사(good이 착한이라는 뜻으로 사용되었음) 뒤
　　에는 of+목적격을 씁니다.

04 too ~ to = so ~ that 주어 cannot

05 사람을 칭찬하는 의미를 갖는 형용사(nice 가 친절한이라는 뜻으로
　　사용되었음)는 for가 아닌 of를 씁니다.

06 be good at 명사/동명사: ~를 잘하다

07 forget to~ : ~할 것을 잊다

08 분사구문/ 나는 돈이 없어서(원인), 반지를 살 수 없습니다.

09 진행형의 분사구문에서는 being을 생략합니다.

10 look forward to ~ing, 이때 to는 부정사가 아니라 전치사입니다.

12 as는 원인을 나타내는 접속사입니다./ 나는 음식이 없었기 때문에
　　당신에게 아무것도 줄 수 없었습니다. 주절이 과거(couldn't give)이
　　므로, 부사절도 과거(had)입니다.

13 must의 과거형은 had to입니다.

14 can의 과거형은 could 또는 was/were able to입니다.

15 must의 미래형은 will have to입니다.

16 can의 미래형은 will be able to입니다.

17 get used to ~ing: ~에 익숙해지다

18 The ship은 단수이므로 단수동사 has가 오고, 수동태 표현 been
　　built가 옵니다.

19 drive-drove-driven

20 분사구문에서 대명사(he)는 고유명사(Billy)로 바꿔야 합니다.

21 현재완료진행형: has/have+been+~ing 과거완료: had+~ed

22 too ~to = so ~that 주어 cannot

23 something+형용사+to 부정사- / something+to 부정사

24 be known to: ~에게 알려지다

25 과거를 나타내는 수동태: was/were+P.P

종/합/문/제 2

p.216~221

01 ③   02 ⑤   03 ④   04 ⑤   05 ③   06 to turn in   07 ②   08 ②   09 She has something important to do tomorrow.   10 He has a lot of things to do tomorrow.   11 that he can't   12 that she can   13 ③   14 ①, ④   15 ③   16 ①   17 ①   18 used to be   19 than   20 has been raining, had made   21 had watched   22 going   23 ③   24 was broken by   25 ①

01 stop ~ing: ~하던 것을 멈추다

02 be fond of ~ing: ~을 좋아하다, be proud of ~ing: ~을 자랑스러워하다

03 It~to의 형태에서 부정사 바로 앞에 for+목적격(her)을 써서 의미상의 주어를 나타냅니다. / 사람을 칭찬하는 의미를 갖는 형용사 (wise)는 of+목적격을 씁니다.

05 be busy ~ing: ~하느라 바쁘다

06 forget to: ~하는 것을 잊다

07 stop ~ing: ~하던 것을 멈추다 / cannot help ~ing: ~를 하지 않을 수 없다

08 의문사+to 부정사 = 의문사+주어+should+동사원형

09 something+형용사+to부정사

10 a lot of things+to부정사: ~할 많은 일

11 too ~to = so ~that 주어 cannot

12 ~enough to = so~ that 주어 can

13 분사구문/점심을 먹은 후에(시간), 나는 나갈 것입니다.

14 (Being)은 생략 가능합니다. /어제 Jane은 피곤해서(원인), 일찍 잤다.

15 분사구문. /Jimmy는 일찍 출발해서(원인), 그 곳에 제 시간에 도착할 수 있었습니다.

16 나는 설거지를 하고 있었기 때문에(원인) 그가 들어오는 것을 듣지 못했습니다. 진행형의 분사구문에서는 being을 생략합니다.

17 may well 동사원형: ~하는 것은 당연하다

18 used to be: 과거의 상태

19 would rather A than B: B하느니 차라리 A 하겠다

20 현재완료진행형 has/have been ~ing, 과거완료 had+과거분사

21 생각했습니다(과거-thought), 영화를 봤다고(과거완료-had watched)

22 remember ~ing: ~한 것을 기억하다

23 spend time ~ing: ~하면서 시간을 보내다, talking이 올바른 표현입니다.

24 수동태 표현: was/were 과거분사 by 목적격

25 be surprised at(by): ~에 놀라다

초판 20쇄 인쇄 | 2023년 4월 15일